"Neither a wise man nor a brave man lies down on the tracks of history to wait for the train of the future to run over him."

—Dwight D. Eisenhower, September 22, 1952

A STRING of PEARLS

JENELLE HOVDE

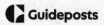

A String of Pearls

Dedicated to Rachelle Kelly-Gonzales, who adores vintage couture and is a blond bombshell in her own right.

CHAPTER ONE

The phone rang, the sound jarring within the silent room. Jack Lund snatched the receiver from the telephone stand and pressed it against his ear.

"Hello," he said, glancing around out of habit to see if anyone might be listening. Gray light filtered through the curtains, barely illuminating his surroundings. The narrow hall and the shadowed kitchen remained silent and empty, despite the custard pie his elderly neighbor from apartment 11 had dropped off hours before. She had always insisted on feeding him, sharing what sugar she had, which was nice, since there were rumors the president would ration sugar by the end of the month. Her matchmaking efforts to pair him with the local girls for a date, however, weren't as welcome.

"That you, Jack?" A deep baritone voice reverberated over the line.

"Yes," Jack answered, keeping it brief. His superior wasn't exactly a man who enjoyed social calls or chitchat.

"I want to go over the details of your vacation."

He grimaced as he shoved a hand into the pocket of his woolen pants. The ironing crease was much less crisp thanks to hours and hours of work. Victor Amundson demanded the use of code words when speaking over the party lines, where strangers could eavesdrop. This was anything but a vacation. In fact, Jack couldn't quite remember a trip he'd dreaded more in his ten years working for the agency.

Regardless, he managed to infuse a touch of gaiety into his tone. "Of course. My baggage is ready. You remember Sam and George and all the gang, don't you? The ole boys are raring for a fresh adventure. There's something about those horse ranches and clear skies in California. They'll get a chance to pretend to be real cowboys for once in their lives."

A slight pause from Jack's superior. "Are you bringing Ricky? He's never left the city before. I'm worried about him."

Ricky. Jack inhaled a deep gulp of air as his fingers entwined in the telephone cord. He had endured the grueling tests of West Point as a cadet, had broken an arm while scaling the white-capped mountains in Alaska, and had even run undercover to infiltrate the Italian mafia flaunting their business in New York. Now he was on the cusp of one of the most significant missions of his life. It was situations like these that made a man's career—or broke it.

Jack untangled his fingers from the telephone cord. "Ricky will leave with us this week. I didn't want to make him wait. There's too much angst with his mother at the moment for him to remain where he is."

A whoosh of air flooded the crackling line, as if someone had heaved a great sigh. It was the most emotion Jack had ever heard from his superior. "All right. Ricky will leave with you."

"I'll watch over him as if he were my brother." Jack spoke the assurance, but his heart stuttered with an erratic rhythm. Right now Ricky was hidden in a wooden crate no bigger than a standard trunk, crammed with other similar wooden boxes inside a climate-controlled federal storage facility constantly guarded by none but the most trusted guards.

"I think you should travel light. Don't take the entire gang this time. And don't let Ricky out of your sight. He's a special kid who needs your full attention."

Jack closed his eyes for a moment as his mind made the rapid calculations of train schedules, stops, and final destinations. He had transported six similar boxes this past month. Arthur. Bill. Stephanie. Stephanie had proved to be quite a handful, requiring him to find an art expert and antique dealer who knew how to pack an elegant lady with care and discretion. Each box was labeled with a special name and assigned an innocuous spot in the train's baggage car.

But he had relied on his fellow agents to man the cars. A group of five of them met at the train station and discreetly took positions at the exits, monitoring the passengers, and then slipped onto the trains with newspapers pinned beneath arms and worn attaché cases in hand, as if on business.

It had worked so far with the last several train trips, one of which had led all the way to Fort Knox and underground bunkers tucked away in the most innocuous locations. Why was Victor wavering now? Had he received word of an internal threat? Was there a mole in the organization?

"My friends need to come with—"

"No, Jack. I've made up my mind. You travel with Ricky. Include Chapman, if you must. Travel light and fast, with the cheapest luggage you can find—nothing

too fancy for that rough country—and call me when you get to the ranch."

Victor's voice betrayed the slightest edge. Unusual for a man who had returned with white hair from the First World War and rose with distinction in Washington.

But Ricky—this package was the most important Jack had ever encountered. A cold sweat broke out between his shoulder blades. "Fine. But it's going to be an awfully lonely vacation."

A short chuckle burst from the other side of the line. "Maybe. Let's hope it's relaxing this time, old sport."

As abruptly as the phone call had begun, it ended with a sharp click, leaving Jack licking his dry lips. And then… a softer click, as if someone had heard all they wanted.

Blood thoroughly chilled, Jack hung up the phone. His fingers trembled as he rubbed his chest. His white dress shirt, rolled at the cuffs, was rumpled from hours of planning the so-called trip.

Was the listener merely another nosy neighbor, one of the retired ladies who asked him far too many questions in the downstairs lobby? Or, as Victor feared, was it someone else? Since the Japanese had bombed Pearl Harbor and Germany continued to march deeper into Europe, everything had changed.

Thank goodness for the code words. Mother, *or the* president *of the United States, might not fully appreciate his new moniker, but it had proved to be an effective one. Only a handful of men knew what Jack was organizing and overseeing to the bitter end.*

He dragged a hand down his face as he considered the train schedules departing the next day. He had more phone calls to make. Chapman would be pleased to be included, but there would be plenty of other men who would be disappointed to miss the adventure of a lifetime, even if they didn't know what was in the boxes.

So much weighed on him that his gut ached.

One thing was for certain. He would never allow Ricky to fall into the wrong hands.

CHAPTER TWO

ebbie Albright slid her warm washcloth across the Whistle Stop Café counter where gobs of pink and yellow frosting puddled, and it wasn't yet ten in the morning. Her best friend and business partner, Janet Shaw, had made fresh doughnuts, and that creamy frosting was a siren call to anyone facing another hectic Monday. In the café kitchen, Janet whistled along to Glenn Miller's "A String of Pearls" as it played softly over the radio.

The café had fallen relatively quiet following the early morning rush. An older couple chatted softly in a booth by a window framed with gingham-checked curtains. They shared a pot of breakfast tea and cranberry muffins.

Another woman waited at the counter, studying the chalkboard menu. She sniffed and dropped her gaze to the contents beneath the curved-glass display case. Wearing skinny jeans, a pair of rhinestone-studded boots, and a form-fitting cashmere sweater, she was quite dolled up this morning with artistic makeup, thick eyelashes, and long blond hair in loose but perfect waves.

"Anything calling to you, Gloria?"

Gloria Haverly ran the florist shop downtown. She was in her late thirties or early forties. Like Debbie, she had returned to Dennison to start a business, after working for an upscale boutique in California.

Gloria shook her head. "Do you have anything healthy, like oatmeal with almond milk and acai berries? Or kale and blue algae smoothies?"

Debbie bit the inside of her cheek to keep from laughing or saying something she might regret. She was pretty sure Janet would never allow algae and smoothies to go together. "I've got muffins, scones, and blueberry pie. Janet can whip up an omelet or a breakfast sandwich. She makes the omelets to order, with cheese, onions, ham, peppers, or anything else you have a hankering for."

Gloria grimaced as she tapped her nails on the glass—long nails exquisitely painted with miniature flowers beneath a veneer of gloss. "I suppose a scone will have to do. I really have no time to wait for an omelet."

"It's amazing, and hey, it's got fruit, right?" Debbie offered with a grin, but Gloria didn't smile back.

Resigned, Debbie pulled out a blueberry scone crusted with sugar. Janet didn't skimp on the blueberries, and she had perfected just the right blend of sweet and tart.

Debbie served the scone to Gloria, who didn't even bother to meet Debbie's eye or murmur a polite thank-you.

"Anything to drink?" Debbie prompted.

Gloria stared at the scone, poking at it with her fork as if it were a dead animal. "Tea, herbal. Do you have a blood orange breakfast blend?"

"You're in luck. We do."

As Debbie poured hot water into a teapot and arranged the teacup and spoon, she caught a glimpse of Gloria's face as the woman tasted the scone. Her expression betrayed pure bliss, if only for a split second.

Debbie set the teapot and cup and saucer on Gloria's table just as the bell over the café door jangled. Debbie raised her head and saw a familiar lanky form in blue jeans and a black T-shirt step inside. Greg Connor. Her pulse kicked up a notch as he ran his fingers over a stubborn cowlick. With thick, dark hair and brilliant blue eyes, he exuded a rugged charm.

"Hey, Debbie," he called out when he saw her, his expression brightening.

"Hey, yourself," Debbie answered, glad to see her friend.

Beside Debbie, Gloria straightened as she brushed aside her hair. "Why, it's Greg Connor. I haven't seen you in ages."

Greg cast Gloria a charming grin, as he did with everyone in town. "Nice to see you too, Gloria. I was glad to hear business has been good for you this spring."

"I had a rush at Valentine's Day. You should have seen the roses and carnations that went out to all the lucky ladies. But you know, Greg, I didn't see you in my shop for any red roses."

Greg coughed, his cheeks faintly pink. "Ah, well…"

Debbie cut in to rescue him. "Want some coffee, Greg? I've put a fresh pot on, although I'm afraid you've missed most of the doughnuts after our latest morning dash. I have a few cake varieties left, but I sold everything else."

He nodded as he approached the counter. "Doughnuts and coffee sound great, but actually, I didn't come for that reason."

She set her tray on the counter, surprised. And maybe a bit concerned over his quiet declaration.

He blew out a long breath as he braced both hands on the counter. She noticed tiny flecks of white paint along his tanned knuckles. Nice hands. Strong and capable.

"You seem troubled. Anything I can do to help?" she offered. Their relationship, which had been one of the bright spots in her move back to Dennison after a stressful corporate job, had danced between friendship and something with the potential to be more.

"I actually came in to talk to you, if you have the time," Greg said.

"No problem." She nabbed two cream-colored ceramic mugs and poured the steaming hazelnut brew into both. A pair of glazed maple doughnuts were all that remained of the Monday madness. She slid them onto a plate and checked the clock. They had a few minutes before the lunch rush, and she needed a break.

Janet peered around the corner. She smiled a greeting. "Hey, Greg! Long time no see."

"Wanna join us for a coffee break?" Debbie asked the friend who had helped her fulfill a lifelong dream of running a café in the historic train station.

Janet arched an eyebrow. "I wouldn't mind a caffeine fix." She didn't bother to remove her apron, which covered a pink T-shirt printed with doughnuts.

From her booth, Gloria watched, a tiny frown lining her brow.

Debbie eased into the booth, delighted when Greg slid in beside her, a hint of his spicy cologne wafting toward her. Janet took the opposite bench, giving her a pointed grin, which Debbie ignored.

Greg cleared his throat. "I'm in somewhat of a pickle with the chamber. As you know, we couldn't have the Easter parade or egg hunt last month for the actual holiday due to awful weather. We've rescheduled the festivities for later this month, and I need some volunteers, if you'd be willing to pass the word around. Our parade organizer, Shirley Tussing, had to quit at the last minute. Her daughter is on bed rest with a tough pregnancy, and Shirley has basically moved into her house to help her full-time. No one else has stepped in to fill Shirley's shoes. No one decorates quite like Shirley. Her floats are famous around the area, so her absence leaves a big hole in our committee. We need someone to manage the meetings and oversee the floats, including the chamber of commerce float, and organize the Easter egg hunt after the parade for the kids."

Debbie heard a chair being dragged across the floor before she could register what was happening. She glanced up to see Gloria's wide eyes full of sympathy. "Oh, Greg, that's terrible news about Shirley. I want you to know I'd love to pitch in. Are you helping with the Easter parade this year?"

Of course Greg would be helping. He helped everyone.

Debbie pushed down her mounting frustration. She had no right to tell him who he could and couldn't talk to, but that didn't mean she didn't want to.

As Greg filled in the details of all that needed to be done and the hours spent working with him, Debbie's heart sank a little further. There was no denying the gleam in Gloria's calculating expression. She had to do something...

"I'll lead the committee, Greg," Debbie blurted.

He frowned at her. "Are you sure? You're already so busy. I don't want you to burn out with everything you're juggling."

"It's no trouble. How hard can organizing a parade be? Most of the work is probably already done." She infused lightness into her tone, ignoring the sharp kick under the table from Janet. If Debbie's friend arched her eyebrows any higher, they would shoot right off her forehead.

Greg gently freed his arm from Gloria's grip. "That's great. Thanks, Debbie."

"You can sign me up too." Gloria smiled brightly. "A parade needs the expertise of a florist, and we'll make Dennison shine."

Debbie felt another shot of irritation, but when Greg placed a warm hand on her shoulder, she couldn't help but meet his smile with one of her own. "Thank you, Debbie. I owe you." Then he leaned down, making her heart flutter, and whispered in her ear, "I'm really looking forward to working with you."

He waved goodbye to everyone and thanked Gloria before exiting the café.

Debbie heaved a sigh of relief when a pouting Gloria finally left.

"I sure hope you know what you're doing," Janet muttered under her breath as Debbie cleared the plates from the table. "You can't help everybody. You've got to say no sometimes."

"It's fine. It'll get me out into the community and promote our business. That's a good thing, right? Besides, Greg must be worn out with all of his responsibilities and the boys."

It was an excellent reason to help, not that she needed the excuse.

But in spite of her insistence that she had everything under control, she wasn't entirely prepared for what happened after the lunch rush.

Beatrice Morrow waited at the counter to pick up her take-out order of Denver sandwiches. Her usual sweet smile was nowhere in sight, her brow lined with a frown. She had retired from teaching elementary school after several decades, and Debbie had been one of her students. Today, Beatrice sported a pixie haircut and a sensible denim jacket against the April chill. She leaned over the counter, motioning Debbie to follow suit.

"Debbie, I desperately need your expert advice. It's urgent." Beatrice glanced around the restaurant, her eyes as wide as saucers, before lowering her voice to a stage whisper. "You remember when I told you my nephew came to town to crash for a few months and look for work? He found hidden treasure at my house, and now he won't stop digging in my backyard!"

CHAPTER THREE

Debbie swallowed hard as she stared at Beatrice's hopeful face. Beatrice, who had taught her how to read, was quite possibly one of the nicest elementary teachers Debbie had ever encountered in Dennison.

She strained to come up with a nice way to refuse, since she had so much on her plate already. None came to mind.

Beatrice clutched the take-out bag to her chest. "I know this is last-minute, but I wondered if you might come to my house after work to see for yourself. Richard found a string of exotic pearls, and he insists they came from a train robbery that happened in 1942 right outside of Dennison."

Train robbery? That was news to Debbie, and ridiculously intriguing. She leaned forward, fascinated despite her resolve not to get involved. Then reality kicked in. "Unfortunately, Beatrice, I've volunteered for the rescheduled Easter parade, and this is a busy season at the café."

"I understand." Beatrice sounded crestfallen. "You're a young lady with a booming business. Goodness, I wish Richard was more like you and Janet. I can't even get him to go through the classifieds for work. Let's just say he's a late bloomer."

"What's this about treasure?" Janet asked, emerging from the kitchen behind Debbie.

Beatrice perked up. "You don't know about that bit of history? Back in 1942, when a train left Dennison under the threat of a snowstorm, someone held it up and got away with lots of money and other things. As legend has it, one of the men who robbed the train was eventually caught, but the stolen goods weren't recovered, because the rest of the thieves escaped."

"I've never heard about that," Debbie said, her mind spinning.

"Don't take my word for it. You can read about it in the newspaper archives. My mom was a kid at the time, and she used to tell all kinds of stories about our house, since her mother took in women who volunteered at the canteen. Mom insisted that one of their boarders must have been in cahoots with the robbers. I always thought she said that just to entertain me and my sister. Who would bury treasure in Dennison? Wouldn't the thieves who escaped take their loot with them? But then Richard found something upstairs, along with a note, hidden in one of the antique armoires."

Beatrice took a deep breath and gazed at each of them as if to make sure they were as enthralled with her tale as they had been over her stories when they were her students.

When Debbie couldn't take the suspense any longer, she said, "What did the note say?"

To her dismay, the bell over the door rang, and more customers flooded into the café.

"I guess you'll have to come and see for yourself," Beatrice said as she hefted her take-out bag.

"All right, I'll run over for a few minutes after work, but I can't spare much more time than that," Debbie said.

It would be a quick visit. Nothing more. She'd check out the note, reassure Beatrice, and enjoy a brief visit with her. After all, Beatrice must be lonely in that enormous house of hers. She had never had children of her own, and her love for her irascible nephew was certainly commendable.

But as Debbie waved goodbye to her old friend and former teacher, she had to wonder if diving into the Morrow family affairs might prove to be a mistake.

The Morrow House hovered over the rest of the houses on the street. Painted green with white gingerbread trim, gabled windows, and a wraparound porch, it stood as a proud throwback to the glory days when the railroad barons ruled the land. Built by a Pennsylvania Railroad officer named Hezekiah Morrow, the house was a symbol of wealth in its heyday. At least until the 1920s, when the stock market imploded and the Morrow fortune vanished overnight. Afterward, the home became a respectable boardinghouse, retaining a classic beauty over the years.

Beatrice had done a fine job keeping up with the old mansion. A series of planters brimming with ferns on the deck and freshly painted shutters framing stained glass windows reflected her efforts to restore the place to its former glory.

Debbie got out of her car and checked her watch. She had just closed the café with Janet, and it had taken longer than usual, thanks to a very busy Monday afternoon. Gravel crunched behind her as Janet's car turned into the driveway. Her best friend had decided she could spare a few minutes to satisfy her curiosity about what was in the note Richard found.

Janet shut her car door, her blond hair blowing freely. Her cute runners and matching pastel T-shirt made her look younger than her forty-three years.

"You're itching for a mystery, Debbie. It's written all over your face."

Debbie chuckled as she peered up at the grand house. "Nah. This is a favor for a friend, right?"

Janet laughed as she shielded her eyes to take in the house and grounds. Debbie followed her gaze. Sure enough, as Beatrice had reported, the garden appeared torn up, with chunks of dirt tossed carelessly on the surrounding grass.

They mounted the porch steps, and Debbie used the brass knocker to announce their arrival. When a young woman with pale blond hair opened the door, the scent of a cinnamon and beeswax candle greeted them.

"Ah, you must be Debbie. I'm Vicky, Beatrice's assistant. I'm so pleased to meet you. I've heard wonderful things about your café."

Debbie and Janet stepped into the grand hall covered in dark green wallpaper. Debbie took in the room, noting the curved oak staircase, the rich oil paintings on the wall, and the lush potted plants on a marble-top table.

Beatrice entered the hall, her face beaming. "Oh, Janet, I'm so glad you came too." She placed a hand on Vicky's shoulder. "Vicky isn't only my assistant. I've hired her to write about the history of this house and my family. She's one of my former students as well. I'm lucky to have her help me write a book."

"That's fantastic, Beatrice. Maybe the depot museum can put the book in the gift shop someday." Debbie smiled at Vicky, who blushed.

"God blessed me with some of the most wonderful students." Beatrice motioned them through double pocket doors into what must have once been the parlor but had been transformed into an entertainment room, complete with a massive TV mounted to the wall above a white mantel.

Beatrice gestured to the black screen covering the dainty wood paneling. "Don't mind my nephew's TV. He says the only place to mount it is over the fireplace."

"How long will he be able to stay?" Janet asked.

Beatrice didn't have a chance to answer before a man entered the room. He looked to be in his midthirties, although his age was difficult to tell because of his long brown hair and beard. He frowned when he saw Debbie and Janet.

"Debbie, Janet, this is my nephew, Richard Carroll. Richard, these women are my former students from the old days, Debbie Albright and Janet Shaw. Why don't you show them the pearls you found? They are amateur historians and run the Whistle Stop Café at the train station."

He mumbled a greeting as he slid his hand into one loose cargo pocket and pulled out a small, rusty tin.

"I found it upstairs in one of the smaller bedrooms near the east wing, which used to house guests," he said, his gaze landing on Debbie.

"It's mostly storage now," Beatrice added. "I hardly go into that room anymore. I've got most of my mother's things stored in those upstairs bedrooms. One of these days, I'm going to have to clean them out—and the attic. Maybe even host a big garage sale if I get the help."

Beatrice's hint appeared to go unnoticed by Richard. He removed the tin's lid and showed Debbie and then Janet the contents. Vicky stepped forward too, her eyes widening at the sight.

Inside the rusted tin lay a necklace of black pearls on a discolored handkerchief, their lustrous gleam catching the afternoon sunlight. Nestled beside them was a folded note yellowed with age.

"May I?" Debbie asked as she held out her hand. Reluctantly, it seemed, Richard placed the tin in her hand. She ran a fingertip over the pearls, the strand cool to the touch.

"Are they real?" Janet asked as she peered over Debbie's shoulder.

"Not sure. If they're fake, they're very good. It's the note that intrigues me," Beatrice replied.

Richard eyed the tin in Debbie's palm. "Of course they're real. Worth quite a lot, judging from the color and weight."

"Go on and read the note," Beatrice urged, ignoring her nephew's protest.

Debbie carefully unfolded the brittle paper. The writing was crisp and clean, with a strong slant, but without a name on either side of the slip.

Forgive me for not settling my account. The pearls are yours to do with as you please.

"Someone must have left the pearls behind as a boarding payment. Seems pretty clear to me. Do you have any idea who might have left them?" Debbie handed the paper to Beatrice.

"As I said, my mother was a little girl during World War II," Beatrice said. "If she were still alive, I'd ask her. She liked to tell stories about the interesting boarders who stayed in the upstairs rooms. Sometimes she would sit in the attic gable, watching the women come and go after dark. She saw someone leave the house the night of the train robbery."

"You should include your mother's childhood observations in your book, Beatrice," Vicky said. "It would be a fascinating addition to your family's history."

"I told you there's treasure hidden somewhere on the grounds," Richard interjected as he crooked a finger at Debbie, silently demanding the pearls.

Debbie held on to them, studying the heavy strand and ignoring Richard. "The necklace is truly lovely, Beatrice. You should get the pearls appraised."

"I agree completely." Richard stepped toward Debbie, a frown lining his forehead. "I've already called an appraiser who wishes to buy the necklace."

Debbie noticed how Beatrice glanced at her nephew with a helpless expression. "I'm not selling them, Richard."

"But they could be worth a lot of money," he argued. "You're just being foolish." The anger that transformed his face was enough to make anyone hesitate, but thankfully, a rap on the front door echoed through the grand hall. Beatrice hurried to get the door and came back accompanied by a young woman with a long brown ponytail and a plastic bin full of cleaning supplies. After a low conversation, Beatrice sent her toward the kitchen.

Richard's attention diverted from the pearls to follow the young woman as she pushed on the door leading to the kitchen. Vicky cleared her throat loudly, drawing his attention back to the group.

"I've hired some help," Beatrice said. "It's too much house to keep up on my own."

"It certainly is," Janet said. "It's an amazing house with an equally amazing history."

Beatrice smiled wistfully. "This house has been in Dennison almost since the beginning of the railroad. It's bound to have a story or two hidden in the walls. Would you care to see the room where Richard discovered the pearls?"

"Unfortunately, I've got to run and make supper for Ian," Janet said as she adjusted her purse strap on her shoulder. Her husband was the chief of police in Dennison. "You kids have fun." She nudged Debbie with a hint of a smile. "But not too much fun, okay? We do have to work tomorrow."

Beatrice led the way out of the parlor. "You should see the balcony on the second floor. I finally got it redone. One of these days I'll add a library to one of the guest bedrooms. Then I want to fix the glass conservatory off the porch."

Debbie's stomach growled—a reminder about needing supper—but Beatrice's pleading expression made her agree to a tour. She sighed at her seeming inability to say the simple word "no."

"Ever think of opening a bed-and-breakfast, Beatrice?" Debbie followed her former teacher up the circular staircase covered with a Persian runner.

"In my younger days, yes. Especially considering how many guests arrive during our tourist season. Maybe I could open for a few select months and hire students to help me with the linens and cleaning. I'm not a baker like Janet, but if you ask Richard, I can make a decent breakfast."

At the mention of his name, Debbie glanced over her shoulder. The young man had disappeared from the parlor.

Beatrice's cell phone rang. She removed it from her pocket and answered. She made no effort to keep Debbie from hearing her side of the conversation.

"Good heavens, no. I am not selling the pearls. My nephew called you, not me. The pearls belong to me. Do you understand? No, Ms. Belanger, I am not interested in your appraising services either. Good day."

Debbie blinked in surprise. She didn't think she'd ever heard sweet-tempered Beatrice speak so sharply.

With a huff, Beatrice jabbed at the screen to end the call and stuffed the phone back into her pocket. "Sorry. That was Cecilia Belanger, the pushy appraiser my nephew is begging me to meet. I keep saying no, but everyone is ignoring me."

"I won't ignore you," Debbie said with a smile. At the landing, she offered the pearls to Beatrice, who shook her head.

"No, I want you to take them for safekeeping. Please, Debbie. Richard is so determined to sell them, even though I don't want to, that I'm worried he might try to do it behind my back. They've been with Morrow House for so long. Why part with them? But as you just overheard, Cecilia won't give up. I'm afraid that if I agree to an appraisal, the next thing I know, I'll have agreed to a sale somehow. I don't want to lose them that way."

Debbie studied the lustrous pearls nestled in the tin can. "I'm no expert on pearls," she said. "Kim might have some answers, since she handles antiques at the depot, but that's not a guarantee. An appraiser might truly be your best bet."

Beatrice frowned. "I agree, but not the one Richard has planned for me. I don't trust people who won't take no for an answer. Will you at least take them to Kim and get her opinion? No one knows more about the history of Dennison than she does. Perhaps her mother could take a peek as well, since she worked as the stationmaster and would have encountered many of the volunteers. I know it isn't likely, but you never know."

Debbie blew out a long breath. "I don't know, Beatrice. I'm not sure I want to be responsible for the pearls."

Beatrice's voice dropped to a whisper. "Please, Debbie. I need you to get them out of my house. Richard is unrelenting,"

"All right," Debbie reluctantly agreed. "I'll take them to Kim in the morning and ask her to talk to Eileen."

With a tremulous smile, Beatrice opened one of the doors off the hallway, revealing mint walls and a large window framed with yellowed lace curtains. Dust motes danced in the bright rays of sunlight, and the room, as Beatrice had said, was full of storage items. A twin bed with a metal frame stood against one wall. A small marble fireplace on the opposite wall held a collection of faded paintings. A pile of hand-knitted blankets and worn quilts perched on the seat of a rocking chair. Other odds and ends included dated brass lamps and an enormous bouquet of silk roses covered in dust.

But the burl wood armoire with its large beveled mirror was what caught Debbie's attention. The piece was almost identical to the one in her own bedroom. She had bought her home from Ray Zink, a kind elderly man who had served overseas in World War II. He had moved to the local nursing home, Good Shepherd Retirement Center. "No one bothered with this armoire until Richard came along," Beatrice said. "He's turning the house upside down, looking for the 'loot,' as he calls it."

The smell of mothballs greeted Debbie when she opened the armoire doors. The interior was in good shape despite the decades of its age and the variety of items heaped about the interior. The belongings inside showed definite signs of having been ransacked, probably by Richard.

Beatrice gestured at the haphazard contents. "See? Richard won't leave my house alone. He's made a mess of my garden, digging everywhere for hidden treasure. But all he's found so far is the necklace."

"Have you asked him to stop?" Debbie stepped to the window, which overlooked the garden, now pitted with large holes. Beyond the garden stood an old icehouse, the roof covered with sod and grass. It appeared ready to collapse at any moment.

Beatrice sighed. "I asked him to stop digging in the garden, but if he won't, what can I do? He's all the family I have left. And I'm all he has too. I can't throw out my sister's son. He needs me. I'm thrilled he has a passion for history, but I wish he would apply some of that fire to finding a proper job instead of going after a get-rich-quick scheme." She patted Debbie's arm. "I appreciate you asking Kim about the pearls. That's one less mess for me to deal with."

Debbie carefully tucked the tin into her jacket pocket. One quick visit with Kim to check the pearls couldn't hurt, could it? After all, how could she say no to her elementary teacher?

Later that evening, Debbie's phone dinged over and over with several text messages in rapid succession as she brushed her teeth before heading to bed. She had texted the train station museum director about the pearls, and Kim had agreed to look at them in the morning.

But the phone continued to beep.

Good heavens. When would it stop? With a groan, she picked it up.

Greg requested that she host an Easter committee meeting at her house the following day. She texted a quick reply, volunteering her house as home base for all future meetings.

Janet had sent a series of texts reminding her to place an order for more supplies at the bakery in the morning.

Beatrice had the last message—a cryptic note regarding her nephew. HE'S HUNTING AGAIN, DEBBIE. I DON'T KNOW WHAT TO DO. SAYS HE WANTS TO TAKE UP THE CARPETING NEXT. WHAT DO I SAY TO HIM?

Debbie dragged a hand down her face, and at that moment her phone dinged again.

HI, THIS IS GLORIA. WHAT TIME DO I COME TO YOUR HOUSE FOR THE EASTER MEETING TOMORROW? I HAVE SO MANY IDEAS TO SHARE WITH EVERYONE, AND I CAN'T WAIT TO GET STARTED.

Debbie's groan grew even louder. With a sigh, she answered the texts one by one, including Gloria's.

This was one meeting she dreaded.

CHAPTER FOUR

Outside of Cincinnati, Ohio
January 2, 1942

The train hurtled toward Dennison, Ohio. Relentless. A steel cage Myrtle Cooper would do anything to escape if she could. By evening, she would reach her dreaded destination. And from there? She forced those thoughts away to focus on the window beside her train seat. Gavin Schroeder had purchased her a first-class ticket. Perhaps in an effort to flaunt the oodles of money at his disposal and to keep her in check.

She inhaled a shuddering breath.

The sun melted into a white landscape dotted with bare trees, hay bales, lonely farmsteads, and the occasional village as the train rushed along the tracks. Dennison was a far cry from New York City or Chicago.

If only she could stop the train, disappear into that grove of trees, and never be seen again.

But escape was impossible this day. She touched the back of her hair, now a mousy brown instead of a lustrous white-gold thanks to no longer having access to bleach. But time in the slammer would tarnish any woman. The red scarf wrapped around her head slid down, and she carefully adjusted it, keeping her gaze averted from the other passengers.

A waif of a girl, with a bobbed haircut and holding a patchwork doll, twisted in her seat across the row to gaze at her. A quick pang struck Myrtle. She had a boy. Well, no longer a boy. Her son was seventeen. Big and strapping, like his late father. But unlike his father, Walter had a level head, for which she was grateful.

She waggled her fingers at the girl and forced what she hoped would pass for a friendly smile. Blend in. Blend in. Blend in, *her mind sang in rhythm to the chug-chug of the train. She certainly looked like nothing special these days. No more satin designer gowns studded with crystals in the neckline and tulle sleeves, or svelte woolen suits with silk blouses and crocodile handbags. No more mile-high heels that made her legs compete with any professional dancer's.*

Certainly no more pantsuits in pure black with rugged boots and gloves dyed to match and a custom belt for her tools. Her sole acknowledgment of her prior life was around her neck. The pearls, inky as the night, had belonged to her mother. Myrtle touched her coat, feeling the necklace beneath her fingers. Warmed by her skin, lustrous and heavy, the magnificent strand was tucked safely beneath a worn cotton dress paired with a simple belt and a dingy collar.

She shouldn't have agreed to take the necklace, but her son had insisted.

"You'll need it for wherever you're headed, Mama. Grandma intended the pearls for you. She would want you to have them."

Myrtle had wanted him to sell them and use the money to buy hockey skates or maybe a football jersey and a new ball, but her boy had refused, his bright blue eyes shining with tears. The freckles scattered across his nose brought so many memories of him as a wee little thing.

"Just promise me you'll be good," he had said, his voice husky—part man but also cracking with adolescence.

Just promise me you'll be good.

Well, she wasn't good. She had never been good.

And leaving him with a foster family had been one of the hardest things she had ever endured. It wasn't her choice, but one couldn't argue with a court decree.

Besides, Walter seemed well enough, living in a ram-shackle farmhouse outside of Cleveland with a family of five. Two boys, one sweet girl, and two parents who outshone her parental efforts any day. He had his school. He had new friends. He even got top marks in history and English. The very idea brought a flush of pride.

Which was why Gavin's lies about her son break-ing the law had been so effective. Predictably, she had fallen for the bait and revealed her son's location. She would forever kick herself for listening to her old cohort. For once again being manipulated by him.

And now, as Gavin had taunted over the phone, he owned her. Body and soul. His price for silence? A trip to Dennison with a single week to learn the lay of the land. She had protested that the idea was madness. After all, the national newspapers had plastered her face on the front page for the past month. Her case had fired the imaginations of journalists everywhere.

"Relax, babe. No one could recognize you now," Gavin had sneered.

That, at least, held a grain of truth. Not even Walter had recognized her when she had begged for a secret meeting.

Had the federal penitentiary changed her that much?

The girl leaned over her seat, ignoring her mother's whispered admonishments as she gawked further. Myrtle averted her gaze to stare out the window again.

The train didn't care about her musings. No, it seemed to speed all the faster, leading her straight to her doom.

Dennison, Ohio

Evening had fallen when Pastor Darrel Armstrong parked his car at the Dennison train station. When he was asked to act as the station chaplain, he had agreed without a second thought. Such an opportunity allowed him to pray with the departing soldiers and comfort families in need of hope. It was a meaningful way he could serve his community and aid the war effort.

He cupped his ungloved hands and blew a warm breath against his numb fingers. His breath frosted white as he watched the men and women stream out of the station for the last train. Plump snowflakes fell, caught in the puddle of light from the streetlamps.

Night had already descended, though it was barely six o'clock. Tonight, he felt bone-weary. But whenever his wife, Clara, gently reminded him to retire, he *brushed her off with a smile. He still had the Lord's work to do.*

Besides, he had promised young Harry Franklin a copy of C.S. Lewis's Out of the Silent Planet. *Harry had overhead him talking about the novel and had wanted to know more about the spiritual allegory disguised as a science-fiction adventure. Of course, Darrel loved to talk books with anyone willing to read or discuss them. He picked up his package from the passenger seat and shut the door to his Studebaker. Pinning the hardcover book beneath his arm, he angled his way across the icy surface with cautious steps. Grateful for the new scarf Clara had knitted and his cozy wool overcoat, he stepped onto the station platform.*

Though he was outside, he could easily see inside the building. The golden lights in the main hall cast a warm glow over the white walls and green trim. The blocks of stained glass glowed like jewels, and the sounds of people greeting loved ones brought a smile to his lips.

He loved this train station. It resonated with a sense of life. Of adventure. Of people coming and going, to whom he could minister—if they would let him. It indicated a worthy purpose, chasing away the fear that looming retirement often brought him.

It was good to be needed.

It was good to give.

He immediately spotted Harry. Dressed in a neat uniform and growing like a weed, Harry appeared older than fifteen.

An elderly passenger approached Harry. "Young man, would you help me with my suitcase?"

"Yes ma'am." He hoisted her luggage, and Darrel hid a smile when Harry nodded at him.

"Hello, Pastor." Harry greeted him with a brilliant smile. "Be with you in a minute after I help this lady with her baggage."

"No rush, but I have something for you. I'll wait." Darrel held up the book, pleased when Harry's smile widened.

Darrel found a free spot on the bench and waited despite the chill. Several women needed help with their trunks, keeping Harry busy. But the boy's shift would end soon enough, as would be the case with a few other workers at the station. If any of them needed rides tonight, Darrel would offer his car, no matter what anyone thought about it. He was doing outreach for God, and he wouldn't allow it to be curtailed by small-minded individuals.

He kept himself entertained by watching men and women descend from the train, and wondering about everyone's story. Middle-aged women hurried past him with stylish but modest hats draped with wisps of netting and plumes. A few children yawned, rubbing bleary eyes as mothers collected belongings. Grandparents rushed the platform with arms outstretched in joy. Several young women descended from the car. Soldiers rushed past, pausing to grab a cup of coffee, a sandwich, and a doughnut offered by the Salvation Army volunteers. Older men in suits or overalls, their faces grim or bored or expectant, exited the train.

But one woman caught his attention more than the others.

She was nothing special to look at. She wore a long gray coat, unbuttoned and rather shapeless—almost as if it were a man's. He glimpsed a plain calico dress under the coat, faded from too many washes. Her hair, caught in a severe bun, was mostly hidden under a headscarf. Poor clothes, judging from her scuffed brown heels and lack of mittens or a scarf. But her face...

Darrel leaned forward and studied her. Dark eyebrows slashed over large gray eyes. A pert nose and a thin but pretty mouth devoid of lipstick resembled so many other women's features. None of that mattered. It was her sharp gaze skittering across the crowd and assessing with a shrewdness he wouldn't have expected that captured his attention.

She descended slowly, as if the Dennison pavement presented a river of hot lava. One enormous sigh made her shoulders sink, and then she froze, as if she might change her mind and duck back into the train. A man nudged her from behind, and she grudgingly obliged, moving toward the station. No extra luggage for her, it seemed. Just one small, tattered carpetbag with a missing handle.

She clutched the bag as if it were a shield.

"Is there a taxi?" he heard her ask one of the station volunteers.

The volunteer, an older lady with a harried expression, frowned at her. "There is. It'll cost you about fifty cents to get a ride to the boardinghouse, if that's where you're going. Better hurry and inquire inside. Gabe always has plenty of customers. If he's taken, one of the women at the booth might place a call for you."

The woman blinked as if surprised. She shook her head, her features suddenly pinched and wan.

It was doubtful she had the money. Gabe, a local man, wasn't much of a taxi driver. Darrel stood up from the bench, debating what to do. He didn't give rides to women. The men, yes, but when Clara wasn't with him, he usually tried to be careful with reputations and whatnot.

But this stranger seemed about to collapse from fatigue.

I'll wait a bit. Maybe someone else will help. Dennison is full of good people. Surely someone else will see her need.

Harry joined him, shaking him from his musings. "Pastor, I see a brown package. Is that what I think it is?"

"Yes, it is. I've ordered you your very own copy of Out of the Silent Planet. I hope you enjoy it, and when you've finished, I expect to hear your thoughts. Come to the manse, and my wife will have scones waiting for you."

He always kept an open door, welcoming guests from all backgrounds and walks of life to the church or his home. Clara kept some kind of baked good in the cupboard for that very reason. With both of their sons long out of the house, moved away and with families of their own, life had become rather lonely and stale. He hated feeling useless.

"Yes, sir, I'll be glad to talk it over with you." Harry held the package to his chest. "Thank you."

"Good." Darren nodded. "Does anyone need a ride home?"

Harry glanced over his shoulder. By now, the station was all but empty. "Yes, sir. I know Bill needs a *ride, and Sandy, the ticket booth lady. If you've got room for me, I won't say no either."*

Darrel smiled. He'd drop Sandy off first, then Harry, and then Bill. His car had room for one more.

He looked at the woman, who had sunk on the bench as if to gather strength.

"One second, Harry." Lifting his chin, he strode toward her. "Ma'am, if you don't mind a nosy old man like me, I couldn't help but overhear your need for a taxi." He held out his hand as if he were at church, ready to greet a visitor. "I'm Pastor Darrel Armstrong. I have room in my car for one more. Do you still need a ride?"

She raised her eyes, her expression shadowed. She swallowed hard then said, "How kind of you."

But she did not shake his hand and instead tightened her grip on the frayed carpet bag.

He stepped back to give her space. He didn't know her story, so he wouldn't take offense. But he would still show her kindness and generosity, which never did anyone any harm. "All right. The boardinghouse? Or perhaps a family in town?"

She shivered. "I've no family and know of no boardinghouse."

"The Snodgrass house is nice enough, but it's not very quiet. And there's the possibility it will be full at

this late hour. Have you considered Morrow House? Esmé Morrow boards respectable women at her establishment. It's a lovely home, historic in the area. Quite affordable too. In fact, another woman I'm offering a ride to stays there."

Her eyes widened a fraction, and then she rose from the chair. "I would prefer quiet."

He smiled at her. Any further efforts on his part to draw her out were met with guarded one-word answers. But he managed to learn her name. Myrtle Cooper.

Sandy, Bill, and Harry joined them, chatting happily, and they all headed as one group to his Studebaker waiting in the parking lot.

Myrtle kept quiet, muttering a flat hello when Darrel made introductions. As he opened the car door and helped her in, he wondered about her past. Especially when her gaze kept drifting back to the train station.

CHAPTER FIVE

As Debbie parked at the depot the next day, she realized that she had forgotten to bring the pearls for Kim to assess. She thought about going back home to get them, but it was Tuesday, and the Dennison Ladies Book Club was scheduled to meet at the café for Janet's cinnamon buns and coffee while discussing their latest read. She didn't have time to retrieve the pearls.

The hours raced by as Debbie and Janet hustled, serving doughnuts and breakfast sandwiches then tomato soup and grilled cheese. The simple sandwich and soup combination had turned out to be one of the most popular daily specials, bringing in a steady stream of customers.

When the clock indicated closing time, Debbie heaved a sigh of relief and stretched her aching back.

"You agreed to host the Easter committee meeting at your house?" Janet shook her head as she removed her apron. Her latest baking T-shirt, hot pink with sprinkles, read, BAKING IS MY THERAPY. "You must be out of your mind. I've been on this committee for three years. It's not a walk in the park."

"I definitely am out of my mind. I even volunteered to host future meetings." Debbie grinned. "But honestly, it's not a big deal. It's just me at the house. I've got lots of room, and I can make coffee."

"You know better than most how long meetings can run." Janet reached into the display case and removed the last of the cookies. "When was the last evening you had to yourself for downtime? I mean *real* downtime."

Debbie winced. It had been a long time. And after her corporate career, she certainly knew how long and tedious meetings could be, with everyone demanding a chance to be heard. "I'll keep it short. I'm sure everyone has a lot to do. They won't want to overstay their welcome."

"I'll bring cookies," Janet said as she slid the oatmeal raisin and chocolate chip cookies into a large pastry box.

"I said I didn't want anyone to linger, Janet," Debbie teased.

Janet winked. "Keep their mouths full of treats, and no one will want to talk. Problem solved."

Debbie laughed. "That's why I love you, my friend."

Running a café with her best friend had to be one of the best decisions Debbie had ever made. They were a great team, and with Janet at the parade committee meeting, things were certain to be entertaining.

A familiar figure popped into the café. Kim Smith, the director of the train museum located in the station, waved a greeting. With her short brown hair in stylish waves, Kim looked the part in a white blouse and chinos, even after contending earlier with a school bus load of fourth-grade students on a class trip.

"Did you bring the pearls, Debbie? I'm sorry I haven't seen you all day."

Debbie shook her head, her cheeks heating. It wasn't like her to forget things. "No, I'll bring them tomorrow. I'm so sorry. I forgot, and now I'll have to let Beatrice know. I'm embarrassed."

Kim waved away the concern, her expression sympathetic. "It happens to the best of us. Don't worry. I'll pencil you in for early tomorrow morning, and we'll take a peek together. Does Beatrice have any idea who might have left the note?"

"None whatsoever. And on top of all of it, her nephew is convinced that a treasure is hiding somewhere in Dennison. He's searching Beatrice's property and not being very respectful about it. Do you know anything about a train robbery outside of Dennison in 1942?"

Kim's eyes sparkled. "I do. Mom wasn't stationmaster at the time, but she was there, and she told me about it. The railroad ordered extra security around the depot after the incident. They were afraid it was the work of an enemy spy. Many stationmasters feared an act of sabotage that might derail the train cars."

"But the US never had an invasion," Janet protested.

"We didn't *allow* an invasion, but there were certainly Nazi spies who tried to infiltrate. They never got through though, because our government remained on high alert after Japan attacked Pearl Harbor. The train robbery, however, proved to be quite a mystery. No one knew exactly what happened to the items stolen from the cargo car. I haven't researched it yet, thanks to my crazy schedule. There's so much incredible history to uncover in Dennison. You never know exactly what you'll find."

A shiver rippled through Debbie as she considered the idea of enemy spies. The history certainly was fascinating—not that she could afford to dive into it now, considering her endless to-do list.

"Maybe you could give Beatrice a rough idea of the value and the name of an appraiser you trust to assess the pearls? From what she tells me, her nephew is planning to sell them whether she wants him to or not. He has an appraiser who's being aggressive about buying them."

Kim frowned. "That's not right. The pearls were found in her house. She should be free to make her own decisions about them."

There wasn't much Debbie could do if Beatrice allowed her nephew to walk all over her. She would bring the pearls tomorrow and get an answer for Beatrice while keeping the necklace out of Richard's grasp. Hopefully, Beatrice would find the strength to give her nephew a solid rebuttal the next time he asked to tear up her carpets.

That evening, Debbie changed into jeans and a dark green T-shirt. The top was casual but pretty, with delicate shirring at the sleeves. She donned a pair of gold hoop earrings and added a dash of lipstick and fresh mascara. All the while, she thought of the perfectly manicured Gloria arriving in a cloud of perfume.

"It's a meeting. How hard can it be?" Debbie murmured to herself.

She descended her newly renovated staircase, done in a Craftsman style with a simple elegance she adored, as the doorbell rang. In the months following Debbie's purchase of the house, Greg had worked on the renovations, updating the historic home into a peaceful refuge.

She opened the door to greet Greg, who held a manila envelope. "Am I the first one?"

"Yes, you are. But I have to warn you. I don't have any sugary treats yet. Janet is bringing the cookies."

He regarded her with that charming smile, his blue eyes sparkling. "That's fine. I'm glad to catch up with you, Debbie."

She stepped aside so he could enter the house. He shrugged out of his jacket, handsome in jeans and a blue polo shirt.

She took his jacket, hung it on the coatrack, and motioned him toward the kitchen. "I'm glad for that too. Want something to drink?"

When he didn't respond, she paused and faced him.

His expression had clouded over. "Debbie, I'm so sorry about the last-minute meeting. I wasn't thinking when I suggested your house. I shouldn't have brought my troubles to you about the Easter festivities. I can help build floats and renovate houses, but I'm no organizer, and I'm certainly no decorator. I felt lost, so when you offered to help, I took you up on it without thinking about how busy you already are."

She smiled at him. "Everyone's busy, Greg. I'm happy to take some of this off your shoulders. What's in the envelope?"

His face cleared. "This is the information that Shirley collected regarding forms for businesses to enter their floats, the fees, the list of judges, and the supplies that need to be purchased—like the plastic eggs. She's already done most of this stuff. The eggs are at her house. But really, if this is too much, I'll find someone else to take on the project."

She opened her fridge and removed cans of soda. "It's no trouble, Greg. I know life is wild for you too. And I love this town. I want to help."

Dare she admit aloud that she liked spending time with him? Would that be too forward?

Unfortunately, the doorbell rang, erasing her chance.

"I'll get it," Greg murmured, leaving her to retrieve a tray of cheese and olives she had picked up from the grocery store on her way home. She carried it, a basket of crackers, and the tray of drinks and glasses to the living room and placed them on the coffee table as Greg opened the door.

Gloria stood in the doorway with a huge grin on her face. "Greg Connor. Aren't you going to let me in?"

"Hi, Gloria—" Greg dodged an awkward attempt at a hug.

The rest of the guests pouring in felt like a blur to Debbie. Everyone cheered when Janet arrived with the cookies. Despite the lighthearted banter and laughter, Debbie swallowed hard, her ire mounting when Gloria squeezed in next to Greg on the couch.

"Your house is so cute, Debbie. I absolutely adore anything old and Victorian," Gloria said as her gaze swept the room.

"It's Craftsman style," Debbie corrected with a slight smile. "And thank you. I owe it to Greg and my dad for the renovations."

Gloria's eyes widened. "Is that so?" She patted Greg's arm. "Beautiful work. Maybe I need to hire you for some odd jobs."

Janet, who sat in a club chair opposite Debbie, rolled her eyes.

"I'm pretty busy," Greg said. "But I can check my schedule. It'll depend on what you need done."

Debbie cleared her throat loudly and called the meeting to order. A feat that proved difficult, since everyone had plenty of questions and kept interrupting each other.

Rose Thebault, a brown-skinned woman with salt-and-pepper curls, folded her arms across her chest. "Will we have a chamber float this year? If so, I want it to be fun for the kids. We could cover a trailer with giant carrots and have an Easter bunny throw candy. Someone will need to do some painting. No big deal, right? Buy some orange and green paint and—"

Debbie rubbed her dry eyes that burned with fatigue. It seemed like no one wanted to take responsibility for anything except Greg, who volunteered to build the float, and Janet, who raised her hand to organize the food booths. The rest of the night followed suit, with plenty of discussion going back and forth, including from Gloria, who protested loudly that any float she contributed to must be drenched in flowers, even if they were of the silk variety.

Which wasn't a bad idea and earned the praise of everyone, including Debbie.

The doorbell rang again, and Debbie hurried to answer it. She opened the door to see Vicky, Beatrice's assistant and ghostwriter.

Vicky had both her hands jammed into her pockets, her expression contrite. "I'm so sorry to bother you. I would have called, but I don't have your phone number. I didn't realize you were having a party." She gestured behind her at the committee members' vehicles.

"It's not a party. It's a meeting to plan the Easter festivities for Dennison."

Vicky looked puzzled, but she didn't comment or question why Dennison was having Easter goings-on after the holiday was long past. "I know I'm pulling you away from something important, but I wondered if I could talk to you about Beatrice. She's not eating or sleeping much. Her desire to write an account of the past, Richard's treasure hunt—it's all been so hard on her. I want to thank you personally for looking into her case. Have you heard anything new about the pearls? Did Kim discover anything about them that might be useful for our book?"

Debbie flushed as she shifted in the doorway, keeping her voice low so that no one else would overhear. "No, I haven't heard anything. And I need to take the pearls to Kim in the morning. I'm so sorry. Work has been crazy."

Vicky held up a hand. "Say no more. I totally understand. Hey, do you need any help with the parade? I've got some spare time on my hands. I'd love to contribute."

"Come on in." Debbie motioned for Vicky to follow. She offered quick introductions, disturbed to see that Gloria had now moved to the kitchen with Greg. From what Debbie could hear, she was asking to see his cabinetry work. Had she roped Greg into giving her a tour of the house? Debbie bristled at the idea.

The doorbell rang again, drawing Debbie back to the front door. She opened it, and there stood a middle-aged woman she had never seen before. She was tall and brunette with chunky glasses lined with rhinestones. She wore a cream-colored wool coat over cream-colored slacks. Even her boots matched her outfit.

"Are you Debbie Albright?" the woman asked with a distinct accent.

"Yes." Debbie didn't budge from the doorway.

"I'm Cecilia Belanger, an appraiser of antique art and fine jewelry. Forgive me for bothering you at home, but I understand from Richard Carroll that you have a necklace which might interest me. I'd love to see those pearls, if you don't mind. Beatrice sent me over—"

"Did she?" Debbie interrupted, remembering Beatrice's desire to evade the appraiser. "Because she hasn't said a single word to me about any such visit, and I don't have the authority to show something of hers to anyone she hasn't asked me to."

Cecilia pushed her glasses up the bridge of her nose. "Now, now, there's no need to get snippy. Richard certainly wants them appraised and considered for purchase. Did you know he has power of attorney over Beatrice's affairs?"

"Unfortunately, I can't simply take your word for that. I would need to see the paperwork, especially since Beatrice is more than capable of determining her own affairs. In the meantime, I will follow her instructions to the letter." Had Richard misrepresented his relationship with his aunt to the appraiser? The thought brought a chill.

The woman scowled as she rummaged through her purse. "I'm a collector based in Cincinnati, and I travel all over the United States for rare items. My expertise is jewelry. Antique jewelry." She removed a card, the marbleized exterior glossy and lined with gold, and handed it to Debbie. "Encourage Beatrice to call me. She won't be disappointed. I offer very fair prices, and my items have been sold at high-end auction houses all over the country. I want pieces with a story. Last year I found a farmer with a prehistoric arrowhead collection in his barn. He never knew what was hiding beneath the moldy hay all those years. Half a million dollars' worth of arrowheads, Ms. Albright. So let's not be difficult with the pearls, shall we? It's not in Beatrice's best interest."

Debbie couldn't shake the uncomfortable feeling the appraiser gave her. Beatrice was right. The woman came across as pushy, to the point of being unprofessional. There was no way Debbie would let her see the pearls without Beatrice's express permission.

"I understand where you're coming from, but unfortunately my hands are tied until Beatrice says otherwise. I can't help you with anything else. Good night, Ms. Belanger."

A shout rippled through the house followed by the sound of breaking glass.

"Oh dear! Do be careful!" shrieked one of the committee members.

Ignoring Cecilia's shocked expression, Debbie slammed the door shut and rushed toward the noise. A teapot lay shattered on the hardwood floor of her kitchen.

Gloria stood there with an odd look on her face. "I'm so sorry. I thought you wouldn't mind if I helped myself to some tea. But the handle felt greasy, and it was slippery…" She gave a little shrug and hastily left the room.

Had Debbie been a lesser woman, she might have lost her temper. Instead, she swallowed her retort and found the broom and dustpan in the closet to sweep up the mess. Her eyes watered when she recognized the delicate rose pattern in shards on the floor. It wasn't an expensive item, but it had been a gift from her mother, an heirloom piece passed down through her family. It was gone, with no chance of repair.

A steady hand rested on her shoulder, and she turned around. Greg peered into her eyes, his expression concerned. "Debbie?"

"It was my mother's teapot," she managed, too overwhelmed to say more.

He hissed in sympathy. "This meeting has been an absolute disaster. Let me clean it up for you, please. It's the least I can do." He gently tugged the dustpan from her hand and took the broom while she struggled to compose herself.

Voices argued in the living and dining rooms, rising in pitch.

Debbie's ire rose a notch, along with the noise. She walked out of the kitchen to see Rose arguing with Agatha Wilson about where to hold the Easter egg hunt.

"McCluskey Park, of course!" Agatha jutted out her chin while folding her arms across her chest, mirroring Rose's stance. "It's big enough for the kids to run and play."

"We did it there last year," Rose snapped. "Let's try something new. Why must it always be your way, Agatha? Who made you the boss of Easter?"

Agatha squared her shoulders. "I will not sit here and take your insults. But you raise a good point. Why wasn't I asked to lead? I've been on this committee for five years, yet not one of you called to ask me to take over."

Debbie abruptly turned and walked back into the kitchen. "I'm not sure any of us can get a grip on this meeting," she said to Greg.

He poured the china fragments into the garbage can. "Actually, I'm surprised by their behavior. They aren't usually this cranky. A little stuck in their ways, yes. Rude, never. I'm almost done here, and then I'll go rein them in."

She glanced toward the living room. Tired as she was from the day's hectic pace and the evening's upheaval, this was her home, she was the chairperson, and she should be the one to intervene. "Thanks for cleaning up the china. I'll see if I can tackle the mess in the living room."

Standing straight and tall, she marched into the fray. "Ladies, it sounds like we've gotten off track with this meeting. Let's at least take turns stating our concerns and opinions. We need to hear each other out and collectively think through the best solutions for the town rather than our own personal pride."

Rose and Agatha retreated into sullen silence while shooting glares at each other.

"Let's vote where to hold the egg hunt," Debbie suggested. "Rose, Agatha, why don't each of you lay out your argument for your chosen location, and then we'll discuss it and take a vote?"

As Agatha began to speak, more calmly than before, Debbie looked around. She was startled to find that Cecilia had entered the house and was standing in the dining room, looking at the knickknacks in Debbie's hutch. The woman made eye contact and hurriedly snatched at some papers in her purse. "I wanted to show you my credentials, but I can see this is a terrible time. Forgive my intrusion."

"Of course." Debbie saw Cecilia out and shut the door firmly behind her, sliding the lock into place before returning to the living room. She didn't buy the credentials excuse for a minute. What was the real reason Cecilia had come into her home uninvited?

The conversation droned on, and Debbie finally checked the time. How was it nine o'clock already? It felt so much later, and yet all they'd agreed on was a carrot float with a bunny suit.

She held up a hand, stopping the debate. "I think you've both made your points. Everyone, raise your hand if you want to have the Easter egg hunt at McCluskey Park."

To her relief, the committee agreed to hold the event at the park. Then they decided who would design the posters and hand out the flyers.

"I nominate Debbie to wear the bunny suit," Gloria called from the kitchen, where she was refilling her drink. She returned to the gathering, and she seemed far too pleased with herself for her comment to be construed as innocent. "I've got one I can lend you. What's your size, Debbie?"

Debbie could only stare at her, horrified.

Janet came to her rescue. "All right, everyone. This has been a productive meeting, but as you know, I have to get up in the wee hours of the dawn to bake while many of you are sleeping, and Debbie has to be at the café plenty early. I think we should thank our host and call it a night. We'll meet again to discuss the details. Maybe next Wednesday evening."

"I agree. And I think we'll move future meetings to the chamber of commerce building," Greg announced. "Honestly, I should have thought of that in the first place, since this is a chamber event and I'm the chamber president. Let's thank Debbie and get out of her hair."

God bless Janet and Greg. Debbie couldn't imagine hosting another meeting like this one.

The guests slowly filtered out, Rose and Agatha still bickering, until only Greg, Janet, and Gloria remained. Greg took his coat from the coatrack and leaned toward Debbie. She caught a whiff of his cologne, light and spicy. "You want to catch dinner sometime this week? We can brainstorm some more about the Easter festivities."

Her mouth dried at his nearness. "Dinner sounds lovely."

Someone coughed loudly behind them. Gloria folded her arms across her chest, waiting to get to her leather jacket.

"So, about those renovations we were discussing, Greg. I'd like to call you and chat further." Her voice was sickly sweet and innocent.

"Yeah, we can do that." Greg rubbed the back of his neck as he regarded Gloria. Was that a flash of disappointment Debbie saw in his eyes?

Steps echoed on the stairs. Vicky blushed as she descended with one hand on the polished banister. "Sorry, I needed a bathroom, and the one downstairs was occupied."

Debbie rubbed her aching temples.

"Thanks for including me in the Easter planning." Vicky grabbed her coat. "And thanks for listening. I know Beatrice will really appreciate your help."

Greg murmured a goodbye and headed out into the night with Gloria close behind him, while Vicky paused, waiting for Janet, who was collecting her purse.

"See you in the morning," Janet told Debbie. "Come on, Vicky. I think you have me blocked in."

Janet steered the younger woman out the door, leaving Debbie with a living room littered with paper plates, warm cheese, and half-eaten crackers.

She shut the door, grateful for the quiet reprieve. Tomorrow would start all too soon.

CHAPTER SIX

O n Wednesday morning, Debbie cracked an eye open and squinted at the clock on her nightstand. Six o'clock.

After getting dressed, putting on her makeup, and brushing her hair, she checked her dresser for the tin box of pearls to take to Kim. It rested on top of an embroidered runner, beside a historical novel she meant to read. Beside the novel, her watch glinted beneath the lamplight.

She slid on her watch and picked up the tin. It felt strangely light. Frowning, she pried open the lid—and gasped.

The pearls were gone.

All that was inside the tin was the note and the yellowed handkerchief that still held the impression where the necklace had been. Gulping, she stirred the handkerchief with her finger, her mind bleary from a lack of coffee. The pearls had to be here. Surely she hadn't lost or misplaced them.

Had she?

A sinking feeling settled in her chest as she lifted the handkerchief from the tin. She had brought the pearls home Monday night after chatting with Beatrice. Dimly, she remembered setting the tin on the console table beside her front door when she'd returned home then carrying it up the stairs to her bedroom when she prepared to go to bed that night.

So where were the pearls?

A thorough search in her bedroom revealed absolutely nothing. Nothing on or in her nightstands. Nothing in her dresser drawers, nor inside her bathroom.

She ran downstairs and rechecked the console, which held a bowl of strawberry hard candies and a box of tissues, but nothing else. Her coat pockets yielded nothing, and her purse held a tube of lip gloss, her keys, a few business cards in a case, a packet of mint gum, and her wallet.

She searched the kitchen she'd cleaned on the verge of exhaustion the night before. She even checked her garbage, rattling the can. No sign of the pearls.

Somehow, she had lost them. But she was *certain* she had brought them home. Last night had proved to be chaotic, with plenty of guests milling through the house. A chill swept through her as she considered each volunteer for the Easter celebration. Had someone stolen Beatrice's pearls?

The sick feeling intensified as she dialed Beatrice before leaving for work.

Beatrice answered immediately despite the early hour, sounding bright and perky. "If it isn't one of my favorite students, up with the sun."

Debbie rubbed the bridge of her nose. A headache had begun to press against her skull, intensified by the conversation she was about to have. "I'm sorry to call so early, but I couldn't wait. You already know I forgot to take the pearls to Kim yesterday. This morning, I grabbed the tin from my dresser to take them to her, and I discovered they're missing. I am so, so sorry. I don't know what happened.

I feel terrible. You trusted me with something important, and I've done nothing but let you down."

Beatrice was silent for a moment, probably digesting the news. Finally, she said, "I'm sorry too, Debbie. I know you wouldn't misplace something carelessly, and it wasn't fair of me to foist them on you in the first place. Perhaps they'll turn up. Let's give it a day or two, okay? There's no need to panic quite yet. After all, they have to be somewhere."

Beatrice's voice, as calm as it had been every day in her classroom, soothed Debbie's churning feelings.

She exhaled slowly as she scanned her bedroom again. "I'm going to keep searching for them. I'll still take the tin and the note to Kim and see what she thinks. And perhaps Eileen will remember the pearls from her days at the depot. They are certainly unusual."

"They are. Richard is furious that I rejected Cecilia's latest offer. I really don't want to let go of anything that belongs to my family at the moment. I can't think straight about any of this, and I feel I haven't had a moment to gather myself, what with Richard treasure hunting all over the house."

"Did you talk to him about the carpets?"

Beatrice chuckled. "Yes. I told him he would have to pay to replace them. That's given me a breather. For now."

Debbie ended the call a few moments later, grateful for her friend's grace. Beatrice showed compassion to everyone in her life, whether stranger, friend or family. A worthy example to follow.

However, Debbie wasn't sure she'd be able to follow her teacher's example if she found out someone had come into her bedroom last night and taken the pearls.

It was opening time when Debbie finally hurried to the café after one last frantic search through her house. She'd even searched her car, although she'd obviously taken the pearls inside, since the tin had been on her dresser. The longer she hunted, the more dread solidified in her stomach as she considered everyone who had come over the previous night.

Tempers had flared between the committee members. Cecilia had come inside uninvited, claiming she wanted to show Debbie some papers. Gloria had broken the teapot, and Vicky had waltzed down the stairs at the end of the night. There was no way of knowing just where people had gone in the house. There had been so much happening and so many distractions, Debbie hadn't been able to keep track of it all.

As she made her way through the depot to the café, she caught up on the Easter committee group text, which had devolved into an argument over whether to include candy with possible allergens. Wasn't there enough chaos in her mind? Finally, she pushed the café door open and was greeted by the aroma of fresh baked treats. Janet had already lined the display case with frosted sugar cookies in the shapes of eggs and chicks. Doughnuts coated in pastel frosting with chocolate sprinkles made Debbie's mouth water. Bless Janet for doing so much on her own. Surely she felt every bit as tired as Debbie did.

Janet came through the kitchen door as Debbie hung her purse on a wall hook. Debbie checked her phone one last time, only to see the screen alight with more texts. Rose was adamant that someone wear the bunny suit and throw candy. Agatha wanted to know who would order the candy for the egg hunt.

Debbie sent one more text, saying she would order the candy. The suit she would continue to refuse, no matter what pressure came her way. Her headache worsened by the second.

Meanwhile, Janet flipped the sign on the door to Open.

"Sorry I'm late," Debbie murmured as she tied her apron.

Janet waved a dismissive hand. "It was your turn to sleep in this week. Sugar cookies are the easiest thing in the world to make."

"One of my favorites." Debbie smiled. However, her excitement faded when Kim entered the café.

The museum director greeted them with a cheerful expression. "Debbie, I'm free to examine the necklace now. I've also found a woman who will assess it. She's a jeweler with expertise in antiques, and her name is Kiki Merriweather. She's excited to take a peek. Honestly, I am too."

Debbie winced. "I can't find the pearls, Kim. I had them at the house, but this morning they were gone from their tin. I had several people over last night to plan the Easter celebration. I don't know if I misplaced them, or..."

She let her voice trail off, not quite able to state her concern that someone had taken them.

Kim's eyebrows shot upward. "Oh, poor Beatrice. That's too bad."

Debbie nodded, feeling her cheeks heat. She pulled the tin from her purse and handed it to Kim. "I've got the container but no pearls. I know I didn't take them out of it. I examined them at Beatrice's house, but that's all. Beatrice would love to know who originally owned the pearls. The note would suggest that someone left them as payment for staying at the Morrow House. I understand her nephew discovered them in an upstairs bedroom, hidden in an antique armoire."

Kim took the tin, carefully opened it, and fingered the handkerchief. She read the note before nestling it back in the case. "I asked Mom about the necklace. She doesn't remember anyone with a strand of black pearls."

"I think we should focus on people who left town suddenly and maybe wanted to keep it secret," Debbie suggested.

"The Morrow House boarded women of all ages and walks of life. The only requirement was that they were of good moral standing," Kim replied as she returned the tin to Debbie.

Someone cleared their throat. Gloria sat at one booth with a cup of coffee and a half-eaten cinnamon roll. She wore her blond hair in a curled ponytail, and her polished nails, bright purple this morning, glinted in the sunlight. Debbie couldn't figure out how she'd gotten in—or how she hadn't noticed her yet.

"She came really early for breakfast, and I didn't have the heart to turn her away," Janet explained under her breath. She smiled brightly and raised her voice. "More coffee, Gloria?"

"Please. With oat milk, if you have it, and make it to go with a blueberry scone." Gloria waggled her fingers from the booth. "By the way, Debbie, I've brought the bunny suit for you. See the box on the booth seat? Can you look after it, please?"

Debbie blinked, her mind moving sluggishly to catch up with Gloria's sparkly exuberance. She glanced at the booth Gloria pointed to and saw a large box with a gigantic blue ear showing through the plastic window on the top.

No. No. No.

While Debbie stood gaping at the box, Janet jumped in. "I've got your order packaged up and ready to go, Gloria. I'll get your coffee."

Gloria rose from the booth, her skinny leggings and long tunic nearly the same purple as her nails. "Thanks, Janet." She wrinkled her nose in a sympathetic grimace, which she aimed toward Debbie. "Kinda seems like you've overloaded your plate. Are you sure you don't want someone else to lead the Easter committee? Sounds like you've got a lot to worry about as it is. Why not stick with wearing the suit and let someone else take over the rest of the planning?"

"I'll be fine," Debbie answered, though she had to strive to keep her tone light. "It'll be over in a few weeks, and we'll all get back to normal."

"I hope you're right. By the way, I just love what Greg did with your place. I can't wait to show him my house. It's got so much potential waiting to be discovered. I've got big plans for Greg Connor. Enormous plans. I'll post photos on my social media for anyone who wants a sneak peek."

"Greg does good work," Kim readily agreed. "He's one of Dennison's best."

"Yes, he is," Gloria all but purred as she gazed at Debbie.

Debbie had to bite the inside of her cheek so she wouldn't say something she would regret. Had Greg really offered to remodel Gloria's entire house? It wasn't as if Debbie could tell him which clients to take and which to refuse, but Gloria's hints about him were wearing thin.

Janet held out a to-go cup and a bag. "Here you go. As ordered."

Gloria took the bag and cup and gave Debbie a playful nudge. "Don't be afraid to ask for help. Good leaders know when to delegate tasks, right? Because if you fail, Debbie, we all fail. Believe me, it won't be a pretty sight."

Debbie's jaw dropped at the well-aimed barb. She racked her mind for an appropriate reply, but Gloria winked and sauntered out of the café before she could come up with one.

Snapping out of her stupor, Debbie grabbed the box with the bunny suit and marched out the door to catch Gloria. "Don't forget your costume."

Gloria opened her car door. "I might not be able to make it to the next meeting because of a doctor's appointment. You know how physicians run late. Can you take the costume and see if someone will wear it? At least have some of the women try it on for size. Thank you ever so much, Debbie. You're the best."

Debbie frowned and began to protest, but Gloria had already shut her car door and started the engine. With a wave, she peeled out of the parking lot.

Debbie returned to the café with the bunny suit, her frown still in place.

Janet pursed her lips and then said, "Don't mind her, Debbie. She's jealous of you. It seems she's after a certain six-foot gentleman who shall remain unnamed."

"I agree," Kim echoed. "Your friends know how hard you work and how capable and dependable you are—although getting help from time to time isn't a bad idea. Nor is resting."

Kim's advice was spot-on, even if it prickled. Debbie glared at the box cradled in her arms. She had no choice but to keep it. For now. She'd take it to the next meeting and find someone else to wear it.

Was the Easter festival headed for mishap? Judging by the number of texts and ballooning demands, Debbie feared the answer to that question.

CHAPTER SEVEN

Dennison, Ohio
January 3, 1942

Myrtle lay on her bed, unable to get comfortable enough to doze off. She closed her eyes, but her attempts to ignore the faint gray dawn peeking through the lace curtains became impossible as night brightened into day.

She rolled over, the bed squeaking in protest. So much remained for her to do that her mind refused to relax enough to allow her to fall into sweet sleep. Lists were her friend. And though she rarely wrote down her lists, her ability to recall the smallest things and categorize everything had proved to be a rare gift.

Her husband had picked up on that talent immediately.

"You remember faces? Numbers? Just like that?" Arnold had quizzed her often during their first month of marriage, after she had recited the winning numbers of the horse races they'd attended as well as the weight and height of each jockey.

"My wife is a walking encyclopedia," he exclaimed with awe. He had paraded her in front of his friends, who came to play cards in the evenings in the stylish penthouse apartment.

She hadn't known it then, but her rich, older husband—who'd courted her with bouquets of roses and hired a violinist to serenade her outside her window at her parents' home—was about to lose everything.

Nor had she known how he earned his money during those years of prohibition and bootlegging. When the speakeasies closed, he had come out on top, even if it meant scraping the bottom of the barrel to add an extra coin to the pile.

Arnold had seen something in her, and he had tended it as carefully as any gardener. It had started small in the beginning. One day he'd said, *"Get dressed up, baby. You're driving me and the guys downtown."* An hour later she stopped the car on his command, and he said, *"Drive the car around the block, doll. Just once or twice. We'll be waiting here for you to pick us up."*

He'd given her a kiss and said, "Don't look so worried. People will think you're going to church."

Except it had been on a Friday, late in the afternoon. And they were sitting in front of the austere steps of a bank.

She pushed away the memory as she swung her feet out from under the worn coverlet and stood. The washstand waited for her, the water cool and refreshing after a restless night. She glanced at herself in the mirror. Her form, still trim after years of ballet dancing and fencing, had lost some of its former strength.

The cold water brought other memories. Federal prison. The never-ending chill, the bleak gray walls of the isolation chamber...

She forced those thoughts aside too.

No, she would never go back to prison. She had escaped it once. Now all she had left to escape was Gavin Schroeder. But her late husband's best friend differed from Arnold in ways that made her skin crawl.

If it hadn't been for Gavin, her husband wouldn't have climbed through the ranks to become number two in a powerful underworld.

One didn't leave Gavin Schroeder. He left you, but not always with your life.

She paused over the washbasin, her fingers twitching. Then the trembling turned into a full-blown shudder. She made herself go over her to-do list, which always had a way of calming her mind and her fingers. She would discover the lay of the land, as Gavin had ordered. She would find work at the train station, investigate the train yard, and learn the security risks, if any. After all, Dennison wasn't New York City or Chicago. She was good at remembering details. She would give a full report back to Gavin as agreed, and he would hold up his end by leaving her son alone for good.

She donned a threadbare dress and stockings then swept her hair up beneath the headscarf. Thanks to the pastor, Darrel Armstrong, she had found a ready welcome at the grand Morrow House.

One would think being surrounded by women would make her feel safer, but she didn't feel safe. Not a bit.

She stepped into the hallway, her modest heels clicking on the hardwood floors. A narrow servants' staircase waited to her left, but she continued on to the grand staircase that curved down to the main floor, the woodwork intricate and freshly polished. Stained glass windows cast a colorful glow on the quaint wallpaper, the detailed paisley patterns bleached by years of sunlight.

Esmé Morrow, the mistress of the house, had explained the history of Morrow House the night *before when she had welcomed Myrtle. Esmé's ancestor, Hezekiah Morrow, had worked for the Pennsylvania Railroad. He'd fallen in love with the Dennison area and ordered this fine house built to impress his young wife from back east.*

Dark wood trim and heavy velvet curtains spoke of a wealth that had vanished during the Depression. But Esmé wasn't one to mourn. "I've got eight bedrooms, each one filled with women," she told Myrtle briskly. "You'll room alone for now, at least until another girl comes in search of work. Everyone needs work these days."

Myrtle hoped no one would stay with her. The bedroom appeared relatively private, overlooking a shabby garden in a quiet corner of the house.

Perhaps the other boardinghouse would have been safer. She could handle men. She had learned to work around Arnold and Gavin. But women intent on chitchat and always asking personal questions? That was another matter entirely.

She needed to be able to carry out her business without being watched too closely.

Her hopes of a quiet breakfast were shattered when she entered the dining room. Esmé hovered over the chipped buffet, placing a collection of mismatched forks and knives. Above Esmé, a massive oil portrait of a white-haired man with a waxed mustache glared down at her. The first Mr. Morrow.

Esmé's smile, however, was far more welcoming. "Aren't you the early riser? I've got scrambled eggs coming. Toast too, with a little jam."

Myrtle offered a wan smile. "Sounds good. But please don't go to any trouble on my account." Her stomach rumbled loudly, contradicting her statement.

Esmé chuckled. "No trouble at all. I like to take care of Pastor Darrel's recommendations. I have him to thank for most of the women boarding at my house. He has quite a knack for sensing who will do well at the station or other businesses in town. Are you planning to find work at the station, or at the drugstore?"

Myrtle pulled out a dining room chair. The back of it was finely carved, though the seat cushion had seen its share of wear. "I was thinking about the station."

"That's a good place to work. We get so many trains passing through these days. I'm sure you'll find a position in no time." Esmé squinted at her. Myrtle's late arrival last night had allowed her to escape nosy questions, especially after she pleaded a headache as an excuse to escape to her room. But she could tell there would be no dodging the landlady's curiosity this morning.

"No family?" Esmé probed as she fussed over the silverware.

Myrtle shook her head, even as an image of her son sprang to mind, bringing a fresh pang.

Fortunately, Esmé didn't press the issue. "Will you have coffee?"

"Tea, if you don't mind."

The breakfast tea was strong and fragrant. Myrtle's cup, though nicked at the handle, retained the gold rim, yet another reminder of better days long gone.

But perhaps this morning's visit wouldn't be entirely useless. Myrtle chose her questions carefully, steering the topic toward the town and the citizens. Esmé seemed glad to answer each of them, often providing more information than necessary as she bustled around the dining room, making sure everything was just so.

"Is there anyone going to the station today I can catch a ride with?" Myrtle asked as she raised her teacup to her lips.

"My eldest daughter, Midge, will take you. But it isn't a terrible walk, even in January. Some of the women walk to work if it isn't too cold."

Walking might be preferable to riding with Midge. If the town was safe enough, Myrtle could wander at will. Maybe even investigate the train yard and determine how far the police station was from the depot.

But she wouldn't refuse a ride today, not with that expectant expression on Esmé's face.

"Whenever your daughter wishes to go, I'd be happy to join her."

"Perfect. If you'll excuse me, I'll finish making those eggs. By the way, the Pittsburgh Press came this morning." *Esmé carried the newspaper from the buffet and handed it to Myrtle.*

All polite speech fled as Myrtle stared at the bold, black headline splattered across the front page. *JAILBREAK! WHERE ON EARTH IS THE BLACK CAT?*

She nearly dropped her teacup, the hot liquid splattering over her wrist. Esmé clucked in concern and dropped a napkin beside Myrtle. Averting her eyes from the nasty headline, Myrtle picked it up and dabbed at her wrist.

"Thank you," *she murmured.*

The headline screamed at her, demanding her full attention, but she kept her gaze on Esmé. She was getting too old for such shenanigans. She had lost her edge over the past two years. The tremble in her hands returned, and she found herself unable to summon a single list to set against it.

Esmé nodded at the paper. "An exciting read this morning about a female criminal. A cat burglar, I believe. I'll refill your cup. You stay put, sweetie."

Truthfully, she wasn't exactly pleased with being nicknamed the Black Cat. She touched her necklace hidden beneath her dress, recalling how Gavin had fingered the black pearls and told her she needed a name that people would remember. But no thief wanted a name or a face. It was far better to be a shadow, clinging to the wall, than to be broadcast to the entire country. With notoriety came the increased risk of capture.

Esmé left the dining room, leaving Myrtle alone with the paper. She snuck a glance at it, almost not believing that the bleached-blond beauty on the front page was her. She barely recognized her younger, glamorous self. She had worn the fitted burgundy suit with a frilly white collar on the advice of her lawyer. Not that he—or the feminine suit—had done her any good. There was no pretending to be respectable after the things she had done.

She folded the paper and rose from her seat to toss it into the nearest wastebasket. Then she hesitated. Throwing it out wouldn't be wise. So, instead, she put it where it had been. Folded, innocuous, and on the buffet for all to see. After all, her husband had often told her to hide in plain sight. "The moment you look guilty, darling? That's when they'll pounce.

Don't quiver. Hold that chin of yours high and pretend all is well with the world, and no one will think twice about you."

She despised his breadcrumbs of advice regarding a life of crime. But he wasn't entirely wrong.

So she resumed her seat at the table and waited for her teacup to be refilled. Just a few more days until Gavin arrived. She could hold out that long—if no one recognized her first.

CHAPTER EIGHT

The next Wednesday night, Debbie pushed open the door to the chamber of commerce building. Janet followed close behind, carrying a box of strawberry doughnuts. They had driven separately but arrived together.

The building, a testament to the old days, featured standard brick walls with a hint of midcentury upgrades. Debbie was happy to travel to the meeting, as she had no desire to host the large gathering at her house again.

Voices carried through the open door of the conference room Greg had reserved for the meeting.

"She didn't!" someone cried out. Debbie recognized Rose's voice.

"Not so loud," someone else hissed. "You don't want everyone to hear you."

"Let's hope the doughnuts sweeten these people up tonight," Janet grumbled.

Debbie smiled at her friend. "You know I believe in your doughnuts, but if your fabulous cookies couldn't work magic…" She let her sentence trail off.

Who knew leading a committee could be so fraught with tension?

Everyone fell silent when Debbie and Janet entered the conference room, the last to arrive. Rose and Agatha were there. Gloria sat beside Greg, having made it to the meeting on time despite insisting she might be running late thanks to a doctor's appointment. The rest of the committee was present as well.

Debbie cleared her throat, disturbed by the smirk curving Gloria's lips. She took a moment to remove her pen and notepad from her purse while Janet doled out doughnuts to the group.

Something didn't feel quite right...or maybe she was jumpy after losing the pearls. Had a member of the group taken them? If so, how could she discover who did it?

And why would no one look her in the eye?

Suddenly, the last thing she felt like doing was organizing any kind of celebration.

But she called the meeting to order. "Why don't we start tonight by picking a theme for the parade?"

"We could call it 'New Beginnings,' as an acknowledgment of the new beginnings we see every spring," Gloria suggested.

Rose scrunched her nose. "That sounds too vague, I think. People could interpret it too many different ways. What about 'Bunnies and Birds'?"

Predictably, Agatha protested Rose's contribution. Finally, everyone voted on the titles, settling on Gloria's idea after Gloria pointed out that multiple interpretations would lead to a greater variety of floats, which would be more interesting to watch.

Debbie scribbled notes, grateful that the strained atmosphere from the beginning of the meeting had dissipated.

Until Gloria once again brought up the idea of Debbie in the bunny suit.

"Someone has to wear it," Gloria said.

Not a single person rose to Gloria's challenge.

"Let's talk about the candy," Debbie cut in, eager to change the subject. "Where did you buy it last year?"

A lively discussion followed on the pros and cons of crunchy, chewy, fruity, and chocolate candies. They finally agreed on what kind to get, and right after that Debbie got herself roped into being one of the judges for the float competition.

She glanced at Janet, who tried to hide a yawn. Neither of them had time to make a float for the Whistle Stop Café, much as they would have loved to have their business represented in the parade. Meanwhile, Gloria took every excuse during the meeting to pat Greg on the arm, laughing brightly.

When seven thirty rolled around, Debbie raised a hand and adjourned the meeting. She still hadn't had supper yet.

"Why are we stopping?" Gloria asked, pouting. "We've got more work to do. I have so many ideas for the Easter egg hunt."

"We'll discuss it at the next meeting. I'll pick up the candy, and maybe we can set up a time to put it in the eggs," Debbie replied firmly. "And we need to decide what to do with the bunny suit."

"Can you continue to store it?" Gloria asked. "I mean, since you already have it and all."

"Yes, that's fine," Debbie said, trying not to sigh.

They arranged to meet again the following week. The group broke up, Janet left, and Debbie stood alone while the others clustered together to chat. None of the women even glanced in her direction, and she felt suddenly ignored and unwanted. As she collected her things, she overhead Gloria talking loudly about how much she appreciated Greg coming over to check out her kitchen, and wasn't he the cutest thing ever?

Fortunately, Greg was preoccupied with Rose's questions about how to build a float quickly and affordably, so he didn't seem to hear Gloria.

Debbie said goodbye, but no one glanced her way other than Greg, who raised his hand in farewell. His blue eyes flickered with an emotion she couldn't decipher, and she was too tired to try.

As she drove home, she mulled over the strange meeting and the way everyone but Greg and Janet seemed to avoid her. Had they somehow found out she'd lost the pearls? But how could they have? Of the people on the committee, only Janet knew about Beatrice's pearls.

Then Debbie's heart sank. *Gloria knows.* She remembered how she'd discussed the missing pearls with Janet and Kim before she realized that Gloria was sitting right there in the café, listening to every word. Did Gloria tell the members of the committee how irresponsible she had been?

But maybe she hadn't been irresponsible. As Debbie drove into her garage, she thought about who had been at her house the night of the meeting and also knew about the pearls. Janet would never take something from her house. Vicky was Beatrice's trusted confidant and assistant. Besides, she would have had plenty of opportunities to take the necklace from the Morrow House. It would have been easier for her to take it from there than from Debbie's house.

Could it have been Gloria? Did she know about the pearls before that morning in the café? The more she thought about Gloria creeping around the house without an invitation, the more disturbed she felt.

To be fair, Gloria hadn't been the only one wandering through her house that night. What about the appraiser, Cecilia, who had come in uninvited under the pretense of wanting to show her credentials? Or Vicky, blushing as she came down the stairs?

Debbie had barely trudged into her house and kicked off her shoes—pausing long enough to nudge them under the console table—when her phone dinged. With a sigh, she realized her work wasn't finished. Everything decided at the meeting had to be carried out within the next few days. Ordering supplies, updating the float entry forms, and booking McCluskey Park. Janet would handle communicating with Ian to block off the parade route.

Debbie picked up her phone to see a message from Greg. ARE YOU OK?

She typed a quick reply. NOT REALLY. EVERYONE BEHAVED SO STRANGELY AT THE MEETING. DO YOU HAVE ANY IDEA WHY?

Her phone rang. "Hey," Greg said when she answered. "I normally wouldn't call so late, but I thought talking would be easier than texting. What's going on?"

"It's fine," Debbie murmured, warmed by his concern. "It was just an odd evening, I guess. Or at least it felt that way to me. Maybe I'm being paranoid or I'm tired or something."

He cleared his throat. "Actually, I picked up on what you're talking about. I think Gloria wants to stir up some trouble. I can't keep all her stories straight. She's angling to be the head of the committee and said you're too distracted. I assured everyone otherwise. Though of course I'd understand if you'd prefer to back out. I don't want to add to your workload, and this is much messier than I anticipated. I never would have asked for your help if I'd known it would be like this."

Debbie shoved a hand through her hair while pressing the phone against her ear. "I'm fine. Truly. But I can't believe Gloria would do something so…so…" She struggled to come up with an accurate way to describe Gloria's actions.

"Middle school?" Greg supplied, his voice tinged with humor. "For the record, you're doing a great job. You're keeping us organized and on task, and that's not easy with this group."

A chuckle escaped Debbie before she sobered. "Good. But…you should know something. I'm embarrassed to admit it, but Beatrice Morrow gave me a string of pearls for safekeeping last week, and, unfortunately, when I got up the day after that disaster of a meeting at my house, the pearls had disappeared. I can't find them anywhere."

She heard a sharp intake of breath from him. "That's terrible. No wonder you were so stressed tonight."

"I don't want to accuse anyone until I know more. But I had a lot of people wandering through my house."

"That makes what Gloria was saying even more strange. She kept hinting about you being, well—"

"What?"

"Less focused than usual?"

He'd probably given her a filtered answer, knowing Gloria.

"I hope she didn't take them."

"She insisted on me giving her a tour of the renovations in your home. I fended her off for the most part, although I did show her the kitchen. It's possible she went upstairs alone when I was busy with someone else. I'm not sure."

A groan escaped Debbie before she could stop it. "Let me know if you hear anything, okay?"

His answer brought a flicker of warmth to her. "You know I will. I've always got your back, Debbie."

"Thank you." She'd take all the support she could get. She had a feeling she'd need it.

CHAPTER NINE

Myrtle waited for Esmé's daughter or anyone else to give her a ride to the station, but Midge complained of a fever, and the Morrow women had to leave Myrtle to her own devices.

She didn't mind. The walk would do her good—and keep her away from prying eyes. After lunch, she dressed as warmly as she could then grabbed her handbag from the small washstand and headed out into the cold. Snow covered the ground, and a recent frost coated the trees like a bridal veil.

She traversed the main street, eyeing the different businesses and noting the services provided even as her mind wandered. The Morrow House had a telephone for boarders' use, so she could communicate with Gavin. She really ought to call him with an update as he demanded, even though she preferred to work alone.

She spotted a park on one side of the street, silent at this time of day, with no children playing in the gathering banks of snow. All of them at school, no doubt, like her Walter. The sign dubbed it MCCLUSKEY PARK, and she was sure it was lovely in warmer weather.

As she picked her way across the icy pavement, she spied a steeple in the distance.

She didn't need to walk to the church. She really needed to find out where the police station was located relative to the train station, but she turned toward the church, her cold feet moving with a will of their own.

The small church was quiet this afternoon, which wasn't surprising for a weekday. Myrtle had every intention of walking past the weathered doors. She hadn't stepped inside a church since she'd married Arnold. Why start now?

But her son's plea resonated in her ears. Please be good.

The white building could use some maintenance. The eaves drooped, and the siding was worn from the harsh Ohio weather. But the stained glass windows were something to admire, likely dating back to the founding of the town.

This must be Pastor Darrel's church. He had been so kind to drop her off at the Morrow House the night before.

She stood on the frosted sidewalk, her fingers aching from the cold. Four years ago, she had worn a luxurious mink coat with a matching hat. Today, a rough wool coat, two sizes too big for her tiny frame, hung on her like a shapeless blanket. The oversize sleeves allowed a draft to creep up her arms.

She shivered and stamped her feet. A few more blocks to walk and she would find herself at the station. She should get moving.

The chill decided her next course of action. Pushing the door open, she entered the sanctuary. A large pipe organ sat on the left, and an upright piano took up space to the right, near the front of the church. Carved wood, polished and cared for, matched the intricate podium. Dim light filtered through the stained glass and cast a rosy glow over the pews. She saw images from the Bible in the glass, detailing scenes of Jesus's life. She recognized them from when she was a girl and her mother had insisted on taking her to church every Sunday.

"May I help you?" a familiar voice asked.

Myrtle whirled around to see the pastor from the night before who had given her a ride with a group of depot employees. The same man who had brought a novel for a young porter after work hours.

Men who did generous things usually exacted a high cost in return.

"It's chilly outside, so I wandered in to see your church. I'm sorry." She folded her arms across her chest.

"We are happy to have people wander in, actually. I have tea in my office, if you would like to warm up." There was a hint of a smile in his voice.

The cynic rose within her. She preferred not to go into a room alone with a man. Pastor or not, he was still a stranger.

"The church is small and less grand than some, but I've always found it charming. I can bring the tea to you here, and you can sit and enjoy the view. As long as you promise not to tell the custodian that I let you have a drink in the sanctuary," he added with a wink. He followed her gaze toward the arched ceiling. "It's a very old church, dating back to the early days of the railroad. It's seen many things. A civil war, the First World War, and now…"

He let his voice trail off, but she knew what he alluded to. Ever since Pearl Harbor had been bombed, so much had changed. Soldiers and volunteers flocked to the train stations. The newspapers were fretting *about the rise of Japan and Germany. When they weren't showcasing her face, anyway.*

"Miss Cooper—"

"Myrtle," she supplied quickly. She didn't bother to correct his assumption regarding her marital status. Arnold Jarman was gone, and she had no intention of tying her name to his ever again. Cooper was her maiden name, and it had felt right to reclaim it. As for Mimi—well, her husband had insisted she needed a glamorous moniker. She much preferred Myrtle.

Pastor Darrel smiled, reminding her of her grandfather on her mother's side. The pastor had gray hair, fuzzy like fleece, and a long nose over his big smile. His rounded spectacles could not hide the joyous twinkle in the blue eyes that regarded her.

"Myrtle," he said slowly, drawing out her name, "is it me, or do I hear a hint of the East Coast in your voice? Boston? New York?"

"Somewhere around there," she murmured before changing the subject. "I wanted to thank you for the ride and the recommendation of a place to stay."

"Have you found the Morrow House to your liking?"

"Yes," she answered.

"Esmé is a friend of mine. You're in good hands with her. She's the kindest soul you'll ever meet."

"Yes, I got that impression. One doesn't encounter such kindness often." The words escaped her before she could retract them. It must be this church and the quiet hush that suffused it. She wasn't used to talking so openly.

Pastor Darrel continued to appraise her, tilting his head as if she were a piece of art to be studied. *"Then you've come to the right place. We care about our neighbors in this town, so we watch out for each other. It doesn't matter what a person's past might be. Only where he or she is headed is important."*

She knew he was inviting her to tell him more. She could see the questions in those keen eyes. And though her mind cried out a warning, her heart rebelled against it.

"Do you truly think a person's past doesn't matter?" she asked.

"I do, as long as there is genuine repentance. It's never too late to begin again with God's help. Redemption is His specialty, after all—taking back the prodigal son who returns. God alone can restore what was lost."

She stuffed her hands into her coat pockets to hide their renewed quiver.

With a slight frown, he rose from the bench. *"Wait here. I have something for you."*

When he returned, he carried a pair of large mittens knitted in alternating blue and white stripes. His own mittens, she suspected from their size. He handed them to her with a quirk to his lips. "My wife knits year-round. I have quite a stash of these."

After a moment's hesitation she accepted the mittens and pulled them over her hands. The wool was warm but not as warm as the kindness in the pastor's expression.

"It is my experience that people cannot change," she said carefully, feeling as if she were walking across a half-frozen lake that was about to crack at any moment.

His gaze remained steady. "People can change, Myrtle. But not on their own. That's why we need God's help. Each one of us. Like the prodigal son, each one of us must return home."

She was done with this conversation. She rose from the bench, eager to leave.

He rose with her. "If you'll forgive an old man's impertinent question, have you found work?"

"I was hoping the train station might have something."

He nodded slowly. "Tell them I sent you."

She kept her tone deliberately light. "How kind of you. How blessed Dennison is to have such a generous reverend."

To her confusion, his expression became sad, and she again felt the piercing of his gaze, as if he were attempting to probe her very soul. "I do what I can and often wish I could do more. My father was a minister also. As far away as New York City, where he tended to the various communities there, especially women in need of escaping particular circumstances."

She stiffened. What a remark. She was bedraggled, but she had never needed a man's help. She had done fine on her own.

But his next comment, so quiet she barely caught it, sent a thrum through her pulse.

"I can't help but wonder, Myrtle, who or what you might be running from?"

January 8, 1942

Darrel headed toward the train station in the evening, this time intent on picking up a specific passenger—his older sister, Hattie, who had planned a last-minute surprise trip.

"I'm planning to stay a few days, and then I'll take the train to Texas to visit Cyril. You won't mind putting up with a sister for a night or two, will you?"

He could hardly tell Hattie no. After all, she was three years older and every bit as bossy as he remembered from their childhood. She had ruled over him and their little brother, Cyril, with an iron hand. But he loved her, and Clara, who had the patience of a saint, was thrilled for company. Hattie promised to stay longer on her way back to New York.

The station was packed this evening, the engines noisy and the whistles sharp. After parking the car, he carefully made his way across the icy road once glazed white, now stained with dirt and travel.

For the past few days, he had puzzled over his conversation with Myrtle in the sanctuary. The way her face had smoothed when he asked what she might be running from. He sensed she was afraid of something. Word had it she had indeed found work at the station, filling in wherever necessary, whether it was cleaning restrooms or learning how to run the ticket booth.

Eileen Turner had told him Myrtle was a quick learner. Quiet, punctual, and unassuming. He had not seen her return to the church since their previous conversation—a thought that continued to unsettle him. Had he said the wrong thing and chased her away?

He found the bench, dusted with fresh snow, but no sign of Hattie. However, Harry was nearby, his cheerful grin for each passenger as he carefully handled bags and hat boxes and anything he could carry from the train. For a fifteen-year-old, he was strong, and his manners were immaculate.

Harry's smile beamed when he spied Darrel. He carried a pair of suitcases, one in each hand, but he paused long enough to say, "Reverend, I read the book you gave me. My mama had to remind me to go to bed at night because I couldn't put it down. It was so good."

"C. S. Lewis's books are unforgettable, whether fiction or nonfiction," Darrel replied. A flush of pleasure from sharing something as simple as a book brought him a renewed sense of joy.

Truthfully, his week had been hard. Some of his flock had suggested that perhaps they needed a younger pastor—one with more vigor and a brood of children—to attract younger families to the pews. The suggestion hurt, even though he reminded himself that such complaints would be inevitable as the years went by. After all, as Clara had gently pointed out again last night, he was past the age of retirement.

Her voice continued to echo in his mind. "We could move closer to the children, Darrel. Think of it. Time with the grandchildren. And we could have warmer weather all the time and never have to shovel snow again."

Dennison was his home, however, and he couldn't imagine leaving it. Even if he had to shovel snow for the rest of his life.

A sigh escaped him in a cloud of white while he waited for his sister.

Harry returned minutes later as Darrel spied Hattie moving inside the train. She was heading toward the exit with the other passengers.

"Reverend, I talked to Miss Cooper last night. She's really nice. I showed her your book, and she showed me your mittens. Seems half of Dennison has gifts from you. You make a mighty fine chaplain for the station, sir."

Darrel chuckled, warmed by the compliment. "Ms. Cooper is well? I haven't seen her lately."

Harry nodded. "She's busy walking all around town. She sure likes the station though. Saw her in the yard earlier, admiring everything. When I went to talk to her, she spun around and said she loved trains. She even asked to climb into the train cars and get a tour, including the baggage car. Said she wanted all the information she could gather in case someone had questions for her at the ticket booth."

Hattie descended the steps, robbing Darrel of a chance to reply to Harry's observations. Hattie spied Darrel and waved a gloved hand. Her fur hat and fur-trimmed wool coat in a vibrant green offered a pleasant contrast to the redbrick station.

"Yoo-hoo!" His sister waggled her fingers.

"That's my sister, Hattie. If you'll excuse me, Harry, we'll have to talk some more about books and other things later this week. I can't wait to hear your insights."

As he approached his sister, another man stepped down from the train behind her. The man paused on the steps and surveyed the area, apparently giving no thought to the passengers standing behind him waiting to get off the train.

The man's face was carved into sharp lines. He turned his head, and Darrel spied a red scar below one ear. A gray suit coat clung to his powerful shoulders, and his gold cuff links winked in the evening's dim winter light, while a luxurious overcoat hung over one arm.

Elegant but dangerous. Very dangerous, Darrel sensed. And Darrel had learned to trust his gut over the years.

Hattie arched her groomed brows as she clutched Darrel's arm. "You hardly seem pleased to see me."

"Oh, I am, Hattie. I'm merely tired these days." He tried to guide his sister away, but the man's gaze roved across the crowd and landed on him. A shiver *rippled through Darrel. He had seen dead eyes before. In New York.*

"Well, it's no wonder at your age. Prancing around town in that car of yours as if you're still a young sapling."

He chuckled, refraining from adding that she too was gallivanting about the countryside, always quick to pursue an adventure at the last moment. Hattie prattled on about the food on the train and the coffee she had ordered at a previous stop that was served cold and with grounds floating on top. But he caught hardly any of it. The stranger had moved off the platform and seemed to be waiting for someone.

And then she appeared. Myrtle pushed the main station door open, pausing midstep when she saw the man. Recognition flared in her eyes, and her mouth pinched.

"Well, well, Mimi, what kind of welcome is this for an old friend?" the man asked as his gaze traveled up and down Myrtle's form.

Mimi?

Darrel frowned. Had he perhaps misheard the stranger?

But Myrtle responded crisply, "You're late," as she stepped farther into the cold. Perhaps Mimi was a nickname, since she obviously knew this man. She wore a simple navy blue dress with a plain white collar, but a gleam of black pearls added a touch of finesse to the plain outfit. Her hair curled beneath her usual scarf.

"Business, darling," the man drawled. "You know how hectic things can get. But I'm here now, and that's all that matters. Did you make arrangements for me?"

Myrtle scowled, transforming her face into something Darrel never would have expected from her. She straightened to her full height, her chin lifted as if in challenge. "There's a boardinghouse nearby, operated by a Mrs. Snodgrass. I've arranged for a car to pick you up any minute."

Their voices dropped below what Darrel could hear for a few seconds, but then the man snapped, "What? You're not staying at the same boardinghouse?"

Myrtle shook her head.

People rushed past Darrel as he watched the couple. Was this Myrtle's husband? Or perhaps a sweetheart? The newcomer had called her Mimi and "darling," yet Darrel could detect no affection for Myrtle in his face. The pastor couldn't tear his gaze away from the troubled woman, though he was vaguely aware that his sister was asking Harry for her luggage.

"Goodness, Darrel, something certainly has you distracted tonight," Hattie protested, patting the curls below her fur hat.

He mumbled appropriate answers to each of Hattie's questions. Yes, Clara would have pie for supper tonight. Yes, the sheets were freshly turned down, and no, it wasn't an inconvenience to host his beloved older sister. Not in the slightest.

A glance over his shoulder revealed that the man had captured Myrtle's hand in his own and he was yanking her farther into the cold. Snowflakes swirled around the station platform, and a gathering chill hinted at a temperature drop. Likely, more precipitation would fall by the end of the night, several inches, if the weather forecast proved correct. Darrel ground to a halt, regardless of his sister's protests.

He was about to spin on his heel and tell the stranger in the fine suit to behave as a gentleman ought, when Myrtle broke free and darted back into the station. The stranger froze and stared after her, as if debating whether to follow.

At least Myrtle would be safe if others surrounded her.

"Darrel!" his sister protested with mild irritation. "What in the world is the matter with you?"

"It's nothing. I saw something that—well, never mind. I'm sure it's nothing." He continued to escort her toward the car, but his mind remained on the station and the stranger.

Who was the dangerous man? And what did he have to do with Myrtle Cooper?

CHAPTER TEN

Two days had passed since the strange commerce meeting. On Friday evening, Debbie sat on her couch, eyeing the mound of applications for the Easter floats. Rose had brought over the folder of forms and basically invited herself to stay for supper. Debbie didn't have anything impressive in her fridge, but she reheated some leftover meat loaf and served it with some green beans from her freezer.

After eating, they reviewed the applications along with the accompanying entrance fees.

"I'll take the money," Rose said, gathering the envelopes. "I'm headed to the bank tomorrow morning anyway."

Debbie readily agreed. After all, Rose was the committee treasurer. But she felt she should offer to help. "If you need me to, I can do it."

Rose frowned. "Nonsense. It's no trouble. You focus on that bakery of yours and making those delicious treats we all love so much."

Debbie chuckled. Janet did almost all the baking, but it was nice to share in the glory.

Seeing a chance to inquire about the pearls, she kept her features neutral. "Rose, I wondered if I might ask for your assistance with something."

Rose paused, her hands hovering over the coffee table and holding a cup of tea. "Yes?"

"I had a black pearl necklace on loan from a friend, and after the meeting I hosted, it was missing. Do you remember seeing anything like it or anything unusual that night? There was so much going on, it was difficult for me to keep track of everything and everyone."

Rose scrunched her nose. "I see. Are you certain you searched everywhere? I often misplace things because I store them in every nook and cranny. My husband gives me such grief for it."

"I remember placing them on my dresser, but I had guests roaming about the rooms, so I'm worried someone moved them."

Rose scowled as she flipped through the forms on the table. "I thought the newer committee members were rather rude. One does not go exploring in another person's house without invitation. I should warn you about Gloria. She was mighty friendly with your Greg. Watch her. She's trouble, pure and simple."

Before Debbie could argue that Greg was hardly hers, Rose said, "You don't think someone took the pearls, do you? One of us?"

Debbie offered a quick prayer for wisdom. "I don't know what to think, Rose. I've turned my house upside down and even went through my car although I remember bringing them inside. But I've found nothing."

"I bet it was Gloria," Rose hissed. "I don't trust her. Not one bit, with those acrylic nails and all that makeup."

Debbie changed the subject. It was one thing to discuss missing jewelry, but another matter entirely to dive into salacious gossip. How Gloria chose to express herself in her appearance was not indicative of her character, which spoke loudly enough for itself. And clearly, Rose did not like Gloria.

The conversation felt increasingly strange even after Rose left, but there wasn't much Debbie could do to figure it out, so she pushed aside the forms cluttering her coffee table. Her phone rang, drawing her attention—a welcome relief.

She answered the phone and was delighted to hear Greg's deep voice.

"Hey, Debbie, are you free?"

She eyed the papers. "I've got a minute."

"I'm sorry about the parade. It's getting out of hand."

"You know how those committee types can be," she joked as she pressed the phone closer to her ear.

"Did you find out anything else about the missing necklace?"

"No, not yet. Rose asked tonight if I suspected any of the committee members."

"I sure hope it isn't one of them. No one has said anything to me." He cleared his throat. "I was wondering if you had any free time this weekend. I realize everyone is probably calling you about the parade…"

She held her breath, waiting for him to finish his thought.

When he spoke again, the words came out in a rush. "I would really like to take you out for dinner. Think you can fit me into your schedule?"

Her heart nearly melted from the vulnerability in his tone. He sounded so hopeful, so wistful. It made her think of high school and dances and all those butterfly feelings she had experienced as a teenager.

"That sounds wonderful," she said, her heart pounding against her rib cage. But then she eyed the papers and her neatly printed to-do list, and reality crushed her plans. "Can we try another time? I've got so much to do in the next couple of days."

"Of course," he replied slowly. "If you need anything, promise me you'll call. I'll do whatever I can to lighten your load."

She grinned. Her heart was officially at puddle status. "I promise."

A low chuckle came from the other side of the phone. "Good. Because I enjoy spending time with you, Debbie Albright. Even if it means playing second fiddle to something you've got on your list."

He knew her well. Her lists were exploding this week. "If I think of something you can help with, I'll let you know," she said.

"I'll await your call."

With a sigh, she said goodbye and got back to the paperwork.

Debbie slid a fresh tray of doughnuts into the glass case as her phone rang. Monday morning had already turned out to be busy, with cinnamon buns and muffins in need of restocking. She picked up her phone as it went to voice mail. A number she didn't recognize flared across the screen.

She returned the call, thinking it might have something to do with the floats or the Easter egg hunt. She couldn't be the committee chairperson and ignore phone calls.

"Debbie? Debbie Albright?" a masculine voice demanded.

"Speaking." She tried to place the voice and failed.

"It's Richard Carroll, Beatrice's nephew. Listen, Aunt Beatrice told me what happened to the pearls. Did you find them yet?"

"Not yet, no. I'm sorry," Debbie answered, her apology thick in her throat—especially at the idea of hurting Beatrice. "I'm hopeful they'll turn up soon."

She heard a heavy sigh. Then Richard said, "I was really wanting to convince my aunt to sell the pearls. She desperately needs the extra money to fix her house. It's in terrible shape. I know she's complained about me wanting to make some changes, but the house hasn't had updates in over thirty years. I've got to fix her roof, which leaks. There's water damage in some of the rooms. I'm hoping there's no mold in the walls. I sure don't have the cash to fix everything for her. And neither does she."

Debbie began to think that Richard could actually be a nice guy. But she changed her mind when he started talking again.

"Because you're my aunt's dear friend, I'm prepared to offer grace and give you a couple of days to find them. But if you can't find them, I may have no choice but to take legal action, and I'd hate to do that to you. The necklace is worth a ton of money, I'm sure. Are you aware that jewelry dealers have appraised South Sea pearl necklaces for up to a hundred thousand dollars?"

She rubbed her forehead, a headache beginning to stab at her temples. "No, I was not aware of that. Are they South Sea pearls?"

"My appraiser thought they were. She was about to purchase them this week, but unfortunately, you talked my aunt out of it, and now she won't get that money."

Had she misunderstood his desire to tear into the house? Was it because he cared for Beatrice and wanted everything up-to-date, or was it because of a legendary treasure?

Guilt held her back from asking. She had no right to question his motives when she had failed to keep the pearls safe for Beatrice.

"I'm sure the pearls will show up soon. I had several people at my house the night before I discovered they were missing, and I've been asking if anyone else saw them."

"Not good enough, Debbie. I'll need you to find them soon. You promised my aunt you would be responsible for them."

She hadn't exactly said she'd be responsible, but she had promised Beatrice to keep the pearls safe—essentially from Richard. If only she had said no to Beatrice's request in the first place and left their family business to them.

Her hands were trembling by the time she ended the call. A quick glance at the café dining room revealed happy customers drinking coffee and eating breakfast. Paulette Connor, Greg's mother, made the rounds with a coffeepot in hand. Paulette often worked part-time, giving Debbie and Janet a breather when the tourist traffic increased.

Thankfully, no new customers stepped into the café. Debbie ducked into the kitchen, inhaling deep gulps of air to control her rising panic.

A hand touched her shoulder. "Debbie, I've never seen you so pale." Janet's nose was splotched with powdered sugar, but it didn't lessen the concern in her gaze.

"Richard claims the pearls are worth an exorbitant sum, maybe even up to a hundred thousand dollars, and he's planning to take legal action." Debbie's words tripped over each other in her eager-ness to spill her troubles to her best friend.

Janet's eyes bulged at the news. "A hundred thousand? That's impossible. Ridiculous!"

"South Sea pearls, I guess."

"I know nothing about vintage pearls, and I'm not questioning their potential value, but I can sniff out a scam when I come across one, and this one stinks. How would Richard be able to estimate their worth when an appraiser hasn't seen them in person? At most he's sent photos to his appraiser, but it would be unethical of her to give an estimate from that."

Her reasoning made sense, and Debbie's anxiety abated some-what, but she still pulled out her phone. "I'm going to call Beatrice. Can you watch the front?"

"You bet."

Debbie dialed Beatrice's number as she tucked herself into the back of the kitchen, where she could talk privately.

Beatrice answered on the first ring and didn't even give Debbie a chance to speak. "Oh honey, I know what you're calling about, and let me say that my nephew's threat is completely uncalled for. For all we know those pearls might be fake. We have no evidence of their true value. None of this makes sense. Believe me, I'm not letting Richard get away with his foolishness. Not when I practically forced you take them for safekeeping and to show them to Kim. He's being way too overprotective of me. Even if we find them, I've decided I'm not sell-ing them. They belong to the history of Morrow House, and they were part of my mother's story. I pulled out her diary and read a few entries.

She remembered a woman with pearls. Why don't we meet and discuss all this? But not at my house, okay?"

"Of course. How about my place tonight? Come over for supper," Debbie suggested. Really, she didn't have a choice, considering Richard's threats. Arrest seemed unlikely, but she simply couldn't afford Richard suing her for that amount. Although Janet was right. An appraiser wouldn't have any real idea of the pearls' value without having seen them. But she couldn't risk it. Dennison was a small town. Word would get out, and her reputation would be destroyed. It could even affect business at the café.

It could ruin her, and worse, ruin Janet. They had both put too much money and effort into the Whistle Stop Café to see it destroyed. Debbie would do whatever it took to avoid that.

CHAPTER ELEVEN

Jack Lund made one last call before leaving his cramped apartment. His worn leather luggage sat by the doorway, each suitcase covered with scratches and gouges. Morning sunshine poured through the small square window above the kitchen sink, highlighting everything with a mellow glow.

The train station awaited, along with his mission.

A woman answered after the first ring, as if she was sitting right next to her phone. Her voice was young and lilting, like a movie star's. "Renee speaking."

He grinned, trying to picture how she might appear. A tall and slender brunette? Or was she blond, with penciled eyebrows and a sweet rosebud mouth? He rather liked her French name and the lilt of her pronunciation. For the past several weeks, he had been in contact with her. If he had the time or the inclination, he would ask her on a date. Of course, that might not be entirely professional, but Renee had proved to be an incredible resource. Smart, funny, discreet. And she could sniff out a Nazi threat like no one else.

In a word, she had become invaluable, and an agent didn't mess with invaluable assets. They were hard to find.

So for now, he would enjoy talking with her during these rare moments. "Did you speak with our gentleman? The one who loves books?"

"Yes," she answered. "He's a willing buyer. I sent out the shipment without a hitch. He'll arrive at the ranch soon. He wants more. Quite the collector."

"Did he give you the names of his friends who also wish to buy?"

She clucked her tongue, the sound almost amusing. "You know how I work. I'm not a used car salesman. I let my clients guide the process. But yes, he has others interested in collecting. They're big. Very, very big, with plenty of cash to throw at me."

That meant overseas players. Had the Germans or the Japanese or the Italians infiltrated Washington so quickly? Were they behind this mess? The urgency to get to the train station rippled through him.

"Sell him whatever you can. Send me the bills, and I'll collect payment."

Her breath shuddered over the line at the meaning of his encoded statement, but she stayed in character even with the concern in her voice. "Please be careful. These are not your average buyers."

He rather liked the idea of her worrying about his safety. But he had dealt with his fair share of rough characters. He was used to "collecting payment."

But then Victor's voice came over the line. "No Wild West theatrics, Lund. Don't be flinging around your muscle when you're on the train or at the ranch. Keep it calm and decorous. I don't want to see a peep in the papers about your exploits."

No guns then. Stealth methods exclusively.

"Yes, sir." He lowered his voice and said, "Don't worry about me, Renee. Just keep me posted."

As he hung up the phone, he wondered if his superior might be asking for too much.

Dennison, Ohio

January 9, 1942

Myrtle stood in front of the local diner. Gavin had demanded she meet him before her evening shift. Like a moth to the flame, she found herself drifting toward *him yet again. And toward certain oblivion. But if it meant continued safety for her son, so be it.*

She waited a moment longer on Grant Street, the charming row of brick buildings a testament to Dennison's glory days of the early railroad. Gold-painted lettering curved along one window of the diner, promising a hot, well-cooked meal. Inhaling a gulp of air, she pushed the door open. To her left, the small dining room offered a homey, cozy view she found charming. After years of elegance that hid a deadly world, she had come to appreciate simplicity, which felt more honest. White tablecloths covered the tables, and small arrangements of silk flowers lined the windows. To her right, a partial wall blocked the view of a smaller room for extra seating.

No sign of Gavin anywhere. Immediately, her shoulders relaxed. A young girl in a white apron over a gray dress poured coffee for a nearby middle-aged couple.

She sank down in the booth nearest the exit, in case she needed to bolt. With her back to the wall, she could observe everyone at a glance. A tip her husband had taught her long ago. Old habits die hard.

The waitress approached her. "Would you like a menu, ma'am?"

"Just tea, and make it scalding, if you please," she answered with a slight smile. Piping-hot tea was useful too. An easy defense should things get out of hand.

No doubt Gavin would come fully armed. Not that he needed weapons. His fighting style had earned him a descriptive nickname in underground bare-knuckle boxing rings—the German Cyclone.

On second thought, perhaps she should order dessert for him. That always had a way of sweetening his mood.

"Do you have any pie?"

"Custard, though it's more water than anything these days," the girl confided in a stage whisper. "Water pie, truth be told."

Myrtle chuckled despite her tingling nerves. Water pie was actually delicious. Made with precious few ingredients, mostly caramelized, and born from the desperate days during the Depression. "Two slices, please."

Before the girl could answer, loud laughter rang from a narrow hallway leading to the kitchen. She cringed, recognizing Gavin's rough voice.

"Go ahead," she told the waitress. "I hear my friend now. If you can, please hurry. He hates to wait for anything."

The girl's eyes widened, but she hurried all the same. Had the poor thing already encountered Gavin's brusque demands?

She hoped he had slept well. He could be a real bear when he was tired or stressed. But the laughter from the hall suggested he was neither. After a moment's hesitation, she left the booth and headed to the edge of the dining room to eavesdrop. He stood with his back toward her beside a telephone mounted on the wall, holding the black receiver to his ear. She heaved a sigh of relief.

His voice was low, but she heard most of his side of the conversation.

"Aren't you a clever girl? How much is the collection worth again? Give it to me straight, sweetheart. You know I love the sound of your voice."

Bile rose in Myrtle's throat, even as she pretended to pat her hair into place, using the large mirror on the wall. The middle-aged couple paid her no heed. Perhaps they thought she was preparing to meet someone for lunch—someone special. She could hardly stomach the idea.

Gavin chuckled again as Myrtle peeked around the corner once more. His back remained toward her, offering a view of the gray pinstripe suit stretched snug across his shoulders. A gold cuff link sparkled on his sleeve. Even his loafers were buffed to a perfect sheen, and his black hair lay in neat, pomaded waves. He shifted as if to turn around, and Myrtle ducked back into the dining room. She should return to the booth, but she had to know who was on the other end of the line.

Who had arranged this deal? What was she stealing? She had so many questions, and Gavin had refused to answer any of them.

"Who knew being a librarian could be so profitable?" he purred. "Remind me to look you up when I arrive in the city. I'll take you somewhere nice, Renee. Somewhere French, eh?"

Fearing the call would end and she would be discovered, Myrtle scurried back to the booth. She had barely resumed her seat when Gavin entered the room.

His eyes brightened when he saw her, and a wicked smile that made her stomach roil curved his mouth.

Thankfully, the waitress arrived at the table, carrying a tray that held a steaming silver teapot, two teacups, and two slices of pie.

Gavin slid into the booth opposite her. "You ordered for me." He sounded pleased.

After the server left, Myrtle nudged her slice of pie toward him, knowing he would devour both pieces. The teapot she claimed, pouring herself a cup. Her fingers felt like jelly, but she gritted her teeth and searched *for some of the pluck that had helped her scale the federal prison wall with nothing but her bare hands.*

No sense in letting fear control her now. That would only invite Gavin's torment. He had always been able to sense when someone was afraid of him, and he had always liked it.

He stared at her. Probing. Assessing. "You seem unwell."

She offered what she hoped was a wry grin. "I have many masks, Gavin. You should know this better than anyone else."

He arched a thick eyebrow. "I do indeed. And now you are a volunteer at the servicemen's canteen."

"I also work at the ticket booth," she told him, keeping her voice low, though the couple had left and the dining room was now empty of everyone but the two of them.

He scanned the room, adopting an air of carelessness. But she knew better. She knew he was on full alert. "What have you found?"

"It's a quiet town. The station employs several young women to work the canteen, but you needn't worry about any of them. They're too busy flirting and eyeing the male passengers. There are also a few porters who are kept on their toes running baggage. The stationmaster manages the schedules and won't present a problem.

The yard is nothing to speak of. It's like any other train yard you've encountered. Low security and preoccupied men. I've even checked the storage cars. They don't lock the baggage compartments."

"What else about the town?"

"Police station is located downtown, about a three-minute drive away. They're not used to trouble here. Like I said, it's quiet. Safe. I don't anticipate any issues for you."

He grabbed his fork and dug into the first slice of pie. It disappeared in a few bites. She tried to ignore the bit of custard clinging to his bottom lip.

He stared at her, his gaze bright and hard. "And you know I need a farm. Have you found one yet?"

She chose her answer carefully. It wouldn't take much to unleash that rage of his. "Finding an abandoned farm has proven far more difficult without a car of my own. However, most of the farms I've seen are small operations with family living on the property. Many of them are likely armed."

"I want a deserted one," he snarled.

She decided to be bold. "I understand, but I need more information so I can be sure to find the right one for you, Gavin. What exactly are we stealing?"

"It's the heist of a lifetime. You and I will quit at the top of our game, and you'll get to live the life of ease *you've always dreamed of. By the way, how is your boy?"*

The tremor came back to her fingers, and she placed them on her lap beneath the table so he wouldn't notice. She fought to keep the tremor from sliding into her voice at his clear threat. "Leave him out of this. He is nothing to you."

"I've got a vested interest in him. After all, he's my best friend's son, isn't he?"

If she begged him to leave Walter alone, it would merely serve to tell him exactly how much her son meant to her—and that would give him more power over her. Power he would use. She shifted the topic. "The details, Gavin. I need them all if I'm going to put my life on the line for you."

He shrugged, though his gaze sharpened on her, as if noticing and cataloging her discomfort. "I've got two other men driving here to meet us. They'll arrive tonight if the roads remain clear of all this blasted snow. Together, we'll all sit down and outline the plans, but not until then."

"If they're bringing a car, I can use it to find your deserted farm." She dared not let him plan too much without her.

"Yes, you can. I'll tell you this much. In a few days, a train will come through Dennison with a special

cargo. We will stop the train after it leaves the station and steal the cargo."

She gaped at him. She couldn't help it, even though she knew firsthand how dangerous it was to show him her true emotions. "You're going to stop a train? How?"

He grinned, revealing a crooked front tooth. "I've got friends in high places. They're arranging a little miracle for me. Believe me, it will stop like clockwork. Everyone will think it's an accident or a breakdown."

"But the train will be full of passengers, including soldiers. How in the world will we arrange such an accident, steal the cargo, and be able to escape?"

He snickered as he pulled the second plate of pie toward himself. "Darling, do you really think I'm stupid enough to give you every single detail right now? You'll be informed when you need to know, and not a second before. In the meantime, enjoy the charms of small-town life. Call that boy of yours, or better yet, I will. Uncle Gavin will have a good word of advice for him on how to catch himself a pretty girl."

She snatched the handle of the teapot before she realized what she was doing. She barely kept her tone as rage and terror pounded through her veins. "Don't you dare contact him again. The feds are watching my son. They fully expect me to run to him. They might even expect you to visit. He's off-limits. You don't need to crow like a rooster. I'm here, and I'll do the job, but if you so much as dial his number, I'll make you regret it."

Gavin pointedly glanced at her hand on the teapot, and an amused smile revealed a dimple in his cheek.

But instead of shrinking, he reached across the table and raised her chin with a stout finger. He smelled of stale coffee and maybe a hint of something vile as he leaned in, locking eyes with her. "You know something? You're quite the dame. Still got plenty of fire in you. And I'm glad Arnold passed on my little hot-tea trick. I've always watched out for you, haven't I?"

She jerked away from his filthy touch. "Knock it off. You men all say the same things, and it's tedious. I'm not a young sapling who bends with the wind every time I hear such nonsense. Nor will you threaten me." She would reach her thirty-sixth birthday this spring, Lord willing. Neither young, nor old. Truthfully, she felt mostly used up, more ash than ember.

He winked as he straightened his garish silk tie. "No? Well, sweetheart, plenty of men want you yet. You, a society girl, who can sashay in those satin gowns. The Black Cat, in those black pants, creeping up the walls—"

"Be quiet," she snapped. "Don't say that name around here. And don't be a fool and jeopardize the gig."

Laughter erupted from him. He was in a fine mood this evening, part devil, part scamp. "Don't worry your pretty little head, baby. You're worth more to me alive than dead or handed over to the feds. I'm never letting you go. You belong to me and me alone."

Her blood chilled at his bold proclamation of ownership. Was this her future, forced to steal on behalf of a man like Gavin, until she was too old to scale a wall or break into a safe? Forced to remain by his side until she was too wrinkled and gray to fill her role as a bombshell burglar?

She had made a youthful, naive mistake when she'd married Arnold and put herself in Gavin's path. Arnold had given her some protection while he was alive, but now she was on her own. Once in the circle of the wolf pack, she could never truly break free of slick men who were full of charm and vice and ruthless brutality. What a fool she had been to think she would be able to escape Gavin's clutches and move forward after this job.

Out of the corner of her eye, she saw a small form approach the table. The waitress. Had the girl overheard her conversation with Gavin? Myrtle hoped not. Gavin wasn't a man to be crossed.

Despite every inch of her longing to kick his shin and distract him from the possible eavesdropper, she refrained from making a scene. But the damage was already done. He spotted the girl, who stared at them with large, velvet eyes, a tray shaking in her hands so hard the dishes on it rattled.

Gavin swung toward the server. "You. Kid. Bring me a pot of coffee. Now."

"Yes, sir." The girl bobbed her head, casting a wide-eyed look at Myrtle, who understood her fear.

"Coffee won't help you," she told Gavin as she edged out of her chair, preparing to make a run for it. "You'd do better to go to bed."

He shook his head with impatience, a lock of hair breaking free of the slick pomade. "Coffee will do just fine. I'm not fooled. I know exactly what's going on, and I know you. Honey, you're not leaving. We're going to wait in this dining room until my friends show up through that door." He jabbed a thick thumb at the entrance. "It won't take more than an hour or two. You don't mind spending quality time with your dear old Gavin, do you? Why, we were friends once."

He grabbed her arm and pushed her back into the booth. She fell into it, her sensible heels turning at the ankles. Moving faster than she would have believed possible, he dropped onto the bench beside her, slinging an arm around her shoulders. It might appear friendly, but she knew he was pinning her in place. The waitress had fled, and the dining room was empty. No help was coming.

She exhaled a small breath. "I can't wait. I've got a shift tonight, and I'd better show up. Otherwise, people will be asking questions you don't want them to ask."

"Here's the deal, Mimi." He leaned forward, his tone suddenly cold and his arm a heavy weight against her neck. "I've got investors lined up all over the world. What you and I are going to pull off will amaze them. Not that you care. You'll be in Mexico, sunbathing on those white beaches, or maybe you'll head to Cuba. You'll be one of the wealthiest women in the world if you play your cards right."

She flinched. If only he didn't know her so well. Had Arnold shared with him about their secret hiding place in Mexico? "Exactly how many packages are you planning to retrieve?"

"I suspect there'll be many. Maybe we can't get them all, but the one I've got in my sights—let's just say it's huge."

She racked her brain, thinking of what might travel on a typical soldier transport train loaded with young men and average passengers. It wasn't as if the Queen of England's royal jewels were being transported through the midwestern United States. What then? Munitions?

She had heard about the disguised trains hurtling through the country, loaded with weapons. Surely such a train wouldn't pass through Dennison, Ohio. No, Gavin's target had to be smaller. More discreet, but just as valuable. Military secrets? A scientist, perhaps? Someone on the run and worth a fortune?

The answer eluded her.

One thing was for certain. Whatever Gavin planned to steal, it would throw her right back into the very world she had fought so hard to escape.

The next morning, Myrtle used the phone at the boardinghouse. Thankfully, she had been given a reprieve last night, fleeing to the safety of the train station, where work awaited her. Gavin couldn't argue with her excuse. But there was no more avoiding it. This afternoon she would meet with the rest of his team at the Snodgrass boardinghouse. Together, they would ride out into the country and find an abandoned farm.

But first, she needed to place a call to her son. The last one, perhaps ever.

Sitting on the small bench with the phone next to it, she was keenly aware of the other women filing in for breakfast despite the early hour.

A boyish voice she knew at once answered after a few rings. "Hello?"

"Sweetheart, it's me." Her throat tightened with emotion. "I know I'm not supposed to call, but I wanted to hear you. Make sure you're all right."

"I'm good. Are you okay?"

She dashed away a tear. "I will be. Remember our conversation at the lake house?" The cottage, if it could be called by such a humble name, had been a rare treat, clinging to the banks of Lake Michigan. Beautiful in the summer and desolate in the winter, with the ice breaking against the rocky shore.

"I remember." Walter's breathing was soft on the other end of the line.

Memories rushed through her mind as she struggled with what to say next. Years prior, in the hush of the dining room of the lake house, right before her arrest, she had told him everything, from his father's crimes to her own sins. Then she'd warned him about Gavin Schroeder and the mafia who might hunt him for revenge.

"You're a good boy," she said. "A wonderful son and my greatest treasure. But there is something I need to tell you. You already know I've done things I'm not proud of, things that would shock you and will continue to hurt you. I'm sorry. So very sorry. I didn't

think I had a choice at the time, but I'd do it differently now if I had the chance. I hope you can understand."

"I understand."

She bit her lower lip until it stopped trembling. "One day you're going to get a call from me and you'll need to hide, the same way I taught you when your father brought his friends to our house. Do you understand? Don't ask questions. Don't linger. Run and hide right away, because your father has enemies who will crush us. I wish I could protect you, but that would put you in more danger. You've got one more year with your foster family. No matter what your foster mother and father say, hide when I tell you to. Tell your foster mother what I've shared with you. She'll hopefully understand and keep you safe."

"But won't you come soon?"

Her heart cracked at the words. "Kiddo, I've been a terrible mother. You deserve so much better."

Walter cleared his throat, the sound a low rumble over the phone. He couldn't disagree with her assessment, but he also refused to hurt her. "My foster family understands. They'll help me."

"Good." Relief rolled through Myrtle, though it was bittersweet. "Don't let any of your father's friends into your life, you hear me? As soon as someone tells you they knew him, you get away from them. It doesn't matter how. No matter what stories they tell you, remember that they lie. Even about me. Don't listen to one word they tell you. I'll be fine. You know I always land on my feet. Focus on yourself, your safety, and your education. All will be well in the end."

"I didn't tell you, but I'm going to enlist in the army as soon as I turn eighteen." He sounded pensive and a touch insecure. "Especially after the bombing of Pearl Harbor, I want to do my duty and help my country. When my foster mom took me to church, the pastor said we should trust our lives to God's care, no matter what the circumstances are. I've been going every single Sunday."

Her heart burst with pride, even if she feared for him. "Good for you. I know you'll do amazing things with your life. I love you, and I'm proud of you."

It was the same blessing her mother had given her. Myrtle touched the pearls at her neck, her mother's gift like an anchor to better memories.

"Mom, I know you're supposed to be in ja—" His voice broke as he cut off the words.

She had never lied to him, and she wouldn't start now. "I know, baby. I've put an awful burden on you. You can report me if you need to. Be honest if someone *asks you questions. And then don't worry. Very few have what it takes to find me. I'm good at what I do."*

"But wouldn't it be better if you turned yourself in?"

She couldn't answer that one, nor could she chide him for speaking so openly on a party line where anyone could listen in. The memory of the gray walls of the penitentiary closed in again, stifling her breath. The feds had convicted her of things she hadn't done, and she bore long sentences for each charge against her, deserved or not.

What if she surrendered right now? Would it all end? Gavin's threats might amount to nothing. But would anyone listen to her? If she could somehow escape Gavin to throw herself at whatever mercy the justice system might provide, what would happen to her son? Gavin would exact a terrible revenge. Walter could hide for a few weeks, but after years of living at a boarding school and now with his foster family, he didn't know how to survive on the run. He was truly an innocent.

She couldn't risk his life. She wouldn't.

"Goodbye, Walter. I want you to remember that I love you always and I'm so very proud of you."

"I love you too, Mom."

The phone call ended with a click. She replaced the receiver and stood, brushing her skirt free of imaginary wrinkles. In the dining room across the hall, Esmé set a platter of scrambled eggs on the table, her keen gaze piercing Myrtle. The older woman stepped out of the dining room. "Would you like some breakfast?"

Her appetite had fled, but it wouldn't be wise to avoid eating. Who knew when she would suddenly need her strength? She forced a smile onto her face. "Yes, please."

"Is everything all right back home?" Esmé asked as she tightened the strings of her cheerful apron, the green fabric bordered with yellow embroidery.

"Yes, everything will be fine. Thank you."

"If you need anything, you'll let me know, won't you?"

Myrtle wished she could speak freely with Esmé, but the longing quickly evaporated. She had never had a trustworthy female confidant, and she couldn't afford to gamble on whether she'd found one now. Instead, she kept the smile pasted on her face, muttered something pleasant, and slipped into the dining room to find a seat at the table.

Esmé's seven-year-old daughter, Louise, sat opposite Myrtle. The little girl grinned, revealing two missing front teeth. In front of her was a plate of half-eaten eggs and a bowl of steaming oatmeal. With her hair in tawny braids and a smattering of freckles, she reminded Myrtle of Walter at that age.

"Why are your eyes so bright this morning, Miss Cooper?" the child asked.

"Are they?" Myrtle touched the corner of her eye and felt wetness. Her heart nearly broke as she recalled the phone call with her boy. She might never see her son again or hear his voice settle into the timbre it would bear for the rest of his life. Regardless of how she felt, she smoothed her features. "I must have some allergies."

But the girl continued to watch her as Myrtle dove into her own plate of fried eggs.

CHAPTER TWELVE

*L*ater that evening, the doorbell rang as Debbie took a steaming tuna casserole from her oven. She set the casserole on the stovetop and discarded her silicone baking mitts to answer the door.

Beatrice didn't smile, although her expression held its usual kindness. "Debbie, bless you for letting me visit."

"It's my pleasure. Come on in. Everything is ready."

Beatrice shrugged out of a denim jacket with sleeves handpainted with brilliant flowers. "I'm relieved to visit with you alone. Richard demanded to know where I was going, but I told him that was my business and to take the night off and leave my carpets alone. He's ruined my armoire by taking it apart. I've got holes all over my yard, and I tripped and twisted my ankle this morning."

Debbie pulled out a dining room chair for Beatrice before returning to the stove to fetch the casserole. Despite the comforting aroma, she had no appetite. "That sounds like he's really looking for something. I'm not an expert on treasure hunts, but he must think he's got a live one."

Beatrice pressed her lips together. "Honey, I know my nephew accused you of losing the pearls, and I want you to know something. I don't believe you simply misplaced them. Not for one minute."

Debbie placed the casserole on a hot pad next to the salad bowl. Her skin prickled in response, all the way to her hairline. "Why do you say that?"

"Because I'm missing something as well. This morning I couldn't find my gold locket. I keep it in my jewelry box. It's special because it holds a picture of my mother when she was a little girl."

Debbie sat down, her mind whirling. "Who would steal something like that?"

"I told Richard about it, and he says I must have misplaced it. But I'm as sharp as ever. Someone is responsible for all of this. I suspect it's the appraiser he's hired, Cecilia Belanger. I've endured several phone calls and an unannounced visit from her. Would you believe she had the audacity to inspect my house and its contents without my permission? Richard gave her a tour."

Debbie thought back to the strange phone call between Beatrice and Cecilia, when Cecilia demanded to see the pearls, and later, her visit the night Debbie hosted the Easter committee. Debbie had found her in the dining room, but who knew where she'd been? It was doubtful anyone would come clean when asked and admit that they had stolen an expensive necklace. "Cecilia came to my house as well. She entered it without my permission after I told her I wasn't going to show her the pearls."

Beatrice threw up her hands. "See? It must be her."

Debbie rubbed the back of her neck. "Your nephew thinks the necklace might be worth up to a hundred thousand dollars. I've got to either find it or find out who has it."

Beatrice patted her arm. "We'll work together. Forgive me for keeping you from your committee work this evening, to say nothing of everything else you have going on, but I want to show you something that goes back to my mother's childhood. I believe the necklace could be connected to the lost treasure of the train robbery."

Debbie held her breath as Beatrice brought out a collection of photographs from her tote bag. Most of the pictures were distorted and blurred with age. Black-and-white, now faded, with splotches marring some of the larger photos.

"My grandmother, Esmé Morrow, was something of an amateur photographer. She took a photo and prayed over each woman who stayed at the boardinghouse. Most of them didn't mind posing for a picture or two. A lot of them volunteered for the war effort and worked in the canteen at the station, cheering the boys as they headed off to war. What a blessing they were. Most of them were proud to serve in any way they could. But my heart nearly stopped when Richard pulled this photo out of the armoire. He was in such a hurry digging for jewelry that he missed the details." Beatrice nudged the photo closer, her finger pointing to one person in particular. "Take a look and tell me what you see."

Debbie picked up the photo, carefully gripping it at the edges so the oil from her fingers wouldn't ruin the finish. A group of women in '40s-style fashion stood side by side, two rows deep, before a fireplace. They were all smiling except for one woman at the back of the group. But it wasn't her unhappy face or uncomfortable stance that grabbed Debbie's attention. It was what she wore around her neck.

"It's the necklace," Beatrice said. "I'm certain of it. And do you know what else is intriguing? Someone took this photo a week before the big train robbery. My grandmother wrote the date on the photograph. What do you think?"

"The necklace and the treasure might have been in town at the same time. If there's a connection between them, and we find the treasure and advertise that we found it, maybe we could lure our necklace thief out of the woodwork," Debbie said slowly.

Beatrice lost some of her enthusiasm. "You think we can find the treasure? After all these years? How can we find it if people have been looking all this time and never found it? And how do we even know what it is that was taken? How do we know what we're looking for?"

Debbie put the photograph down, folded her hands on the table, and smiled at Beatrice. "We have something no one else has. We have a picture of a woman wearing the pearls who left town without paying her bill at your grandmother's boardinghouse—maybe on the same night as the train robbery. Those are clues, my friend. Clues that will lead us to some answers."

Beatrice beamed with approval as she dug into the casserole with her fork. "You are just as smart now as you were thirty-five years ago. I knew I came to the right woman."

Tuesday morning, with a snapshot of the vintage photograph saved on her phone, Debbie pushed the door to the Whistle Stop open. She heard Janet humming in the kitchen, though it was barely six o'clock. When Debbie walked through the door, Janet looked up from smothering a tray of freshly baked cinnamon rolls in cream cheese frosting.

"Did you see what's on the counter out there for you?"

Debbie shook her head.

Janet chuckled as she coated one more roll with gooey frosting. "Go on. Take a peek and tell me if it isn't the sweetest thing you ever saw."

Curious, Debbie obeyed, though she was positively bursting to share her latest discovery with Janet. All protests fled when she saw the gift waiting for her. There, on the glass counter, sat a teapot. A beautiful teapot with yellow flowers and green ivy trailing around the spout, extending to a gold-rimmed lid. It was similar to the one she'd lost at the ill-fated committee meeting.

She picked up the note that accompanied it.

> *Dear Debbie,*
>
> *I wanted you to know how sorry I am about your mom's teapot. I hope you don't mind, but I found one for you at the antique shop in town. It isn't exactly the same, but it made me think of you and spring and sunshine, and I hope you like it anyway. Thank you for all you do and how you serve others. You are amazing, and I look forward to having dinner with you soon.*
>
> *Yours,*
> *Greg*

Debbie held the note a moment longer, absorbing the touching words.

"Oh, he *likes* you." Janet peered over Debbie's shoulder. "He really likes you."

She blushed as she took the teapot to the back, where it would be safe. It had been so many years since her fiancé, Reed, had been killed in Afghanistan. She had never considered finding someone else. Yet Greg had been a good friend since her return to Dennison. He had lost his wife to cancer several years ago, and was raising his teenage sons, Jaxon and Julian, by himself. The idea of a romantic dinner with him made her heart rate kick up a notch. Could there be something more between her and Greg?

Unfortunately, she didn't have a free moment to ponder such a question, but she carefully slid the note into her purse, finding the safest spot to keep it from crumpling. And then, trying to ignore the heat in her cheeks, she helped Janet frost another tray of cinnamon rolls.

Janet allowed her approximately thirty seconds of peace before she burst out with, "Well?"

"Well what?"

"What's going on with you and Greg?"

"We're friends."

"Naturally." Janet nodded sagely. "Plenty of guys give their friends teapots that remind them of 'you and spring and sunshine,' which is also a totally normal thing for a guy to put in a note to a friend."

"He's a particularly considerate guy," Debbie said. "And not to change the subject, but I spoke with Beatrice last night. She's missing another piece of jewelry besides the pearls. I was wondering if we should ask Ian for advice."

Janet paused over her bowl of frosting, the spatula dripping. "Beatrice has had something stolen as well?"

"A gold locket with a childhood picture of her mother. I had so many guests in my house the night before I found the pearls missing. Cecilia, Vicky, Gloria, and the other committee members. The thief could be any of them. I have to figure out who took them."

"I hear what you're saying," Janet said. "But I don't want my best friend to endure any further stress. Don't you think it would be better to let the police handle this? You really don't have to feel responsible for finding the pearls, no matter how much you want to help Beatrice. Good causes are wonderful, but you shouldn't stretch yourself to the breaking point. At a certain point, you owe it to yourself not to take on anything else."

Debbie frowned as Janet's words sank in. "I understand, and normally I'd agree with you. But right now, I have no choice. I have to hunt for the pearls and help Beatrice figure out who left the necklace behind at Morrow House. I can't afford the lawsuit Richard threatened."

Janet blew out a long breath. "Okay, I get it. Tell me what you need. We'll solve this mystery together."

"Thank you." Debbie hugged her friend. She didn't know what she would do without Janet, who had become like a sister to her over the years. They had gone through their childhood and high school years together, laughed and cried through the years of life since, and now they shared the café.

While they filled the display case, Debbie brought Janet up-to-date on what she and Beatrice had discovered the night before.

"Okay." Janet slid the door shut and went to the sink to wash her hands. "So where do we start?"

"I think first we need to identify the woman in the photograph," Debbie said. "We know she was in Dennison the week the train was robbed, and we know she left town suddenly without paying her bill."

"Yes, but we don't know when she left," Janet pointed out. "Just because Beatrice's mother said she saw a woman leave the house the night of the robbery doesn't mean it was this woman. She could have left weeks or even months after the train robbery." She grabbed a towel to dry her hands. "Not to mention that women were coming and going all the time, volunteering at the canteen."

Debbie sighed. "I understand what you're saying, but we've got to start somewhere. Might as well begin with her."

After work, Debbie parked her car at the local library. She headed into the brick building, greeted by the sweet scent of well-loved books. A group of teenagers occupied the head librarian's attentions, discussing the latest reads. Debbie had countless wonderful memories of this library as a child.

She waved at Carol, a young librarian who loved expressing her personality through her clothing as much as Janet did. Wearing a T-shirt that read FULLY BOOKED, Carol waved back, her wispy hair swept up with a gold barrette.

Thankfully, the archival room was free of distractions. Sitting in front of the computer, Debbie hunted for headlines about the train robbery. A quick internet search had revealed several in the 1880s and more in the early part of the twentieth century, the largest of which occurred in June of 1924. With the help of a crooked postal inspector, a crew of four brothers and a few other men tricked a postal service train into stopping then forced the mail clerks aboard to transfer cash and valuables into waiting cars. The take was estimated between two and three million dollars, as such trains often carried enough to cover payroll and other business expenses. Much of it was never recovered. Debbie scrolled through article after article, reading about the robbery itself as well as the trial.

So why was she struggling to find articles about the Dennison robbery? Wasn't that crime newsworthy? Why did only a few papers cover it?

She stared at the article in the January 13, 1942, edition of the *Evening Chronicle*, a local newspaper. TRAIN ROBBERY OUTSIDE OF DENNISON.

Last night, mail bags and cargo were reported missing after an outgoing train halted on the icy track just miles from Dennison. Witnesses noted they saw a car parked on the tracks that forced the train to stop.

Debbie rubbed her chin as she read the rest of the article. The authorities arrested one man, Jimmy Brennan, at the Cleveland train station. He went to federal prison for life. He claimed he had not acted alone.

She leaned forward in her chair, her pulse racing as she considered the black type and the grainy photo of the Dennison train station.

Jimmy listed his accomplices. Gavin Schroeder was still at large, along with another man named Sylvester Alberto, and a woman. Had they taken the items and sold them? Did they hide their loot? Why didn't the paper list a name for the woman? Was she the woman with the necklace from Esmé Morrow's photo? A train full of passengers, including soldiers, experienced a robbery without a single shot fired. And yet only a handful of papers deemed the incident worthy enough to report.

Things didn't add up. The lack of coverage felt unusual. The lost loot should have been a headline story, possibly across the nation.

It was almost as if no one knew or cared about it.

But why?

CHAPTER THIRTEEN

Myrtle kept her pose relaxed in the passenger seat of the car while Gavin drove through the countryside. In the back seat, Jimmy Brennan, a wiry redheaded Irishman, cracked his knobby knuckles. Beside him, Sylvester Alberto repeatedly ran his hand through his wavy black hair.

She didn't like the idea of traveling alone with three men, even in the afternoon, but she needed full control over the farm site. It was better to have her hand in everything and be able to influence Gavin, if possible, rather than let him plan without her. Surprises got people injured—or worse.

The women staying at Esmé's house had provided the solution for her. One shy girl had let it slip that her

*late grandfather had owned an old farm, now aban-
doned since her father's career had taken him else-
where. With her grandfather's recent passing, her
father had posted the land for sale. She had been in
town to care for her grandfather in his last days and
clean out his house, and now she was staying at the
boardinghouse while figuring out her next steps.*

*A miracle, really. Because Myrtle had exhausted
every other option while trying not to appear suspicious to the townspeople.*

*"You did good, Mimi. Real good," Gavin drawled
as they followed a winding gravel lane to a small farm
and a barn. A grove of trees blocked the house from the
road, providing another measure of security. He pulled
the car to a stop and got out, surveying the land.
"Jimmy, you bring the getaway car here. Park it next
to the house as if it belongs and leave the key in the
ignition."*

*How in the world Gavin had secured not one but
two cars was beyond her. The idea of so much cash
floating around in preparation for the crime brought
on a shiver. If Gavin was willing to sink so much into
his plan, it meant he expected a huge return.*

"Cold?" Gavin eyed her with a smirk.

*"It's Ohio in the winter. Of course I'm cold." She
tugged on her woolen mittens. The mittens Pastor*

Darrel had given her. He had become a presence in the back of her mind, like her son.

She could almost hear him telling her, People can change, Myrtle.

No, Pastor, they can't change. I can't change. I've been a thief for far too long. *What was the old saying? A leopard can't change his spots. Certainly, the Black Cat couldn't change hers either.*

She squeezed her fingers into a clumsy fist despite the thick wool and forced herself to memorize her surroundings. It truly was an ideal location, far enough from town that the police wouldn't be monitoring any comings and goings. The farm lay about a hundred yards south of the tracks, so she would need snowshoes to cross the fields. But she was fast, even on snowshoes. Gavin would be with her as they carried away the stolen goods, while Jimmy and Sylvester would distract the passengers on the train.

A simple plan, but one that required precise planning down to the minute or all would be lost.

Gavin's boots crunched on the fresh snow as he headed up the driveway. There were no other tracks, either from feet or from tires, which meant the farm was truly as abandoned as the girl had claimed. Jimmy and Sylvester went to the barn and pushed the door open to peek inside.

She took advantage of the moment to speak to Gavin alone. "You got a lot of money to prepare for this job, Gavin. Who's your backer?"

He sniffed. "Don't ask questions you don't want the answers to, sweetheart. I'm protecting you and your boy. And don't give me that look. The people who hired me aren't fools to be messed with."

"You always know how to find a good payoff, but this sounds like a lot, even for you. Government?"

Had a corrupt senator or business tycoon bribed him?

He grabbed her arm with a tight grip—so tight she nearly gasped from the pain. "I'm not telling you. You'll have to trust me. They'll ruin us if we mess this up. All of us."

"I know the package can't be too big if you've got me running in snowshoes."

"It's big," he cautiously admitted. "But not in the way you think it is."

That meant it probably wasn't military weapons. Something light, like paper or jewels. His admission gave her something to work with.

She pried her arm free. "Jimmy and Sylvester don't mind you and me running from the train and leaving them behind after we rob it?"

Gavin shook his head as snowflakes fell, flecking his gray coat. "It's not as if anyone will suspect them. Jimmy will pretend to have a heart attack or choke on something in the dining car. That'll draw attention away from us. Sylvester will park this car on the railroad as if he's broken down. The train will stop—and distract more people."

"Trains don't stop. They plow right through cars."

"This one will stop. Guaranteed, doll face. When it does, you and I will hightail it to the storage car and grab what we can. So I need you to make sure the snowshoes are in the cargo car and tell me if you see anyone who could be a cop buying a ticket."

He had bribed an engineer to stop the train? The very idea chilled her further. She shoved her hands deeper into her pockets. "We can't leave Jimmy and Sylvester behind with no exit strategy."

"We won't. Sylvester's car will miraculously start, and he'll move it off the tracks. Jimmy will rest and 'recover' in the passenger car once his act ends. They'll meet up with us in a place we've already agreed on. Then we'll have a sit-down with our buyer and—well, that's just the beginning. There'll be plenty of work from now on."

Nausea roiled in her stomach. She would never be free of Gavin. He had said that she would be a wealthy woman after this heist. A woman who could do as she *pleased. Of course, it was all lies. He would keep her chained to his side to appease this mysterious buyer for the rest of her life. Or until her usefulness ran out, which would amount to the same thing.*

"Fair enough," she replied quietly as the cold air swept around her, bringing a fresh smattering of icy snowflakes. The triumphant gleam in his eyes further unsettled her.

In a matter of days, they would rob the train. A train full of rowdy boys, many just a year or two older than Walter. A pang stabbed the center of her chest when she thought about her son planning to enlist on his eighteenth birthday. He had selected a far nobler occupation than she had. And how badly he wanted the same for her. If only her past wasn't so wicked.

No, she couldn't change. There was no path for her to take other than the one that lay before her.

Later that evening, Esmé greeted Myrtle at the boardinghouse door. She eyed Gavin, who remained behind the steering wheel as the car rumbled. At least he had dropped Jimmy and Sylvester off at the hotel first.

But to Esmé's credit, she said nothing as Myrtle entered the house. Myrtle removed her damp coat, the snow melting into it. Then the soggy mittens, which she stuck in the pockets of the coat.

"They'll never dry that way," Esmé scolded. "Go lay them in front of the fireplace."

Myrtle did as she was told, a small smile crossing her face of its own accord.

"Snowstorms are coming," Esmé muttered as she drew a lace curtain back from one of the long windows.

Myrtle glanced over her shoulder, noting a gray sky deepening to indigo hues as night approached. "That won't be good for the trains."

"They run in all kinds of weather unless it's a blizzard—although this storm might become something fierce." Esmé shrugged as she let the curtain drop back into place. "It's the cars and trucks that suffer on those county roads. Get a stout wind, and the drifts will block them."

Terrible news indeed. Gavin wouldn't enjoy hearing about such risks. But she highly doubted he would call anything off unless the blizzard of the century came through and shut down the entire town.

At least there was one thing Gavin Schroeder couldn't control, and that was the weather.

CHAPTER FOURTEEN

aving gleaned all the information she was likely to get, Debbie left the library and made her way to Morrow House, parking behind Janet's car in the driveway. Plenty of tasks related to the Easter celebration waited for her at home, but both she and Janet had promised Beatrice a quick visit. Janet waved to her and exited her car, and the two of them walked up the porch stairs.

Richard scowled at them as he opened the door, his bulky frame, dressed in a superhero T-shirt and baggy jeans, blocking the doorway.

"Beatrice invited us over for coffee and dessert," Debbie announced cheerfully, although she wanted nothing more than to bolt for her car. His accusation still burned. However, she wasn't about to let him see her discomfort.

The silence stretched awkwardly.

Finally, he moved aside, allowing her and Janet to enter the magnificent hallway. Cardboard boxes were scattered across the gleaming hardwood floors. They were full of newspaper clippings and old photos.

"Any news on the treasure hunt?" Janet asked him as she shrugged out of her jacket. The weather remained damp and cool with a light rain.

He grunted. "My aunt is waiting in the parlor."

"Cheerful man," Janet muttered under her breath, while Debbie tried not to grimace. Was he simply an overprotective nephew, as Beatrice claimed? Or was he more obsessed with long-lost loot than his aunt's well-being?

When they reached the entrance to the parlor, framed with exquisite fretwork, Beatrice motioned them closer to the bulky leather couch. "Come in, come in. I found Esmé's records. I want to show you something."

That was an unexpected boon, to be sure, but should Richard be privy to such information? Debbie glanced over her shoulder as he swaggered into the parlor after them. He folded his arms across his thick chest and leaned against one of the tall bookshelves.

Beatrice paid him no mind, and Debbie looked at Janet. Her friend shared Debbie's concerns, judging by the wrinkle in her brow. But the yellowed book Beatrice held was enough of a distraction for Debbie.

Beatrice opened the volume and handed it to Janet. "This is a list of the women who stayed at the house. I'm sure we'll find the signature we need. Let's see if it matches the writing on the note."

"How can we be sure that the woman in the photograph used her real name?" Janet asked as she scanned the faded signatures, most of them displaying elegant penmanship.

"We can't be," Debbie said. "Let's just see what we can find."

"We might be able to narrow down the list if we focus on the weeks leading up to the robbery," Beatrice said as she shuffled through some pictures.

Janet pulled the book closer toward herself, angling it so Debbie could read it as well. "We'll start by looking around January 12, 1942."

"Is there a ledger of some sort that might show when a woman paid her rent and left the house?" Debbie asked.

"I hadn't thought of checking financial records!" Beatrice beamed with delight. "What a great idea. Will you look upstairs in the second bedroom on the left, Debbie? There's a box of books in there I still need to go through. I'm sure you'll find something. The women in my family have always had a hard time getting rid of anything."

"I'll get it," Richard volunteered as Debbie rose from the couch.

"Don't trouble yourself," she responded sweetly. "Maybe you'll see something in your aunt's pictures that will help our search."

Richard appeared torn between the box of photos and going upstairs, but Debbie had already reached the curved banister. Exhaling her relief at escaping his overbearing presence, she jogged up the steps to the bedroom Beatrice had indicated.

To her surprise, Vicky stood in the center of the room, holding one of the aged books. She looked up with a startled expression. Her free hand brushed her pocket.

But before Debbie could ask what she was doing, Vicky recovered her composure and smiled. "Did Beatrice send you up to help hunt for more books about the boardinghouse?"

"She did," Debbie answered. "I'm hunting for some sort of record. Accounts paid, so maybe a ledger of some kind?"

"I haven't seen anything like that yet, but here's a photo album of the Morrow family." Vicky held it out to show Debbie some pictures, including a young girl with pigtails. In one sepia-toned photo, a woman Debbie recognized as Esmé Morrow stood beside a tall, elderly man. He was positioned slightly away from the family, as if Esmé had encouraged him to join the photograph at the last minute.

Despite the plain suit and wisps of white hair, his youthful smile was charming.

"Do you know who that man is?" Debbie asked.

"Pastor Darrel Armstrong. Esmé wrote the names of her family and friends on the back of most of the photos. He pastored that old church on the north side of town."

Debbie vaguely remembered Greg mentioning that church a while ago. Some outside buyer had purchased it and wished to turn it into a youth center, offering after-school programs and other fun activities. Greg and his crew had been hired to renovate it from top to bottom, and bring it up to code. It would be a massive undertaking, but he was excited about it.

"I walked past it the other day. The stained glass windows are stunning. Shipped all the way from England, I understand. Though the rest of it is going to need a lot of work." Vicky held the photo album to her chest. "I'll take this to Beatrice. I'm not sure she's seen it yet. We've cluttered the bedrooms up here with storage boxes full of family history. It'll take months to go through everything."

Debbie felt herself relax. Vicky was a trusted member of Beatrice's inner circle, and she clearly had a burning desire to research history. Who could fault her eagerness to dive into the Morrow legacy?

"When did you start working for Beatrice?" she asked.

"About a month ago," Vicky said over her shoulder as she reached the door. Her free hand strayed to her pocket. "Richard and I were friends when we were kids, and, as you know, Beatrice was one of my teachers."

Interesting... Debbie hadn't realized Vicky was connected to Richard as well as Beatrice.

Debbie walked over to a box of dusty books perched on an old sewing desk. She opened the box and was delighted when she saw the dates on the spine of one of the books it contained. 1941 to 1943. She flipped through the pages, searching for entries from January 1942. Esmé had printed the names of women in neat rows. She had included arrival and departure dates as well as payments. Suddenly one entry jumped out at her. Debbie peered closer at the faint handwriting and sucked in an excited breath. A question mark filled the spot to record the final payment received.

The woman who hadn't made her final payment? *Myrtle Cooper.*

Debbie made her way down the curved staircase with the record book. To her relief, Beatrice and Janet appeared to be alone when she returned to the parlor, both of them poring over the photo albums.

Beatrice glanced up. "Did you find anything of interest?"

Debbie held out the record book, open to the page that had captured her attention. "I did. And I found a woman who didn't settle her bill in January of 1942. Myrtle Cooper. Esmé put a question mark on the ledger. The dates coincide with the train robbery—which also tracks with my recent library excursion. I found an article that claimed a woman took part in the crime although she escaped. No one seemed to know her name, which I thought rather odd. A Gavin Schroeder also evaded capture. I couldn't find anything more about either of them in the papers."

"Myrtle Cooper." Beatrice drew out the name as she studied the page. "Perhaps she's the woman in our picture. The one who left the pearls and the apology. At first glance, I would say the handwriting in the guest book matches the handwriting from the note."

"Why would Myrtle leave such a lovely necklace behind? Especially if she was involved in robbing a train?" Janet flipped through another photo album filled with vintage postcards and pressed flowers.

Debbie wondered as well, but she had other questions too. "I also saw a picture of a man with Esmé. Pastor Darrel Armstrong. Did he have strong connections to your family?"

"Yes, my family loved him dearly. They often said it was hard for any pastor after him to fill his shoes. He had such a heart for hurting people, often helping those in need. He and his wife regularly came to the Morrow House to minister and meet with the guests. You'll find him in many of the old photos. The Armstrongs were so influential that several of the women who boarded with my grandmother went to church on Sunday for the morning service and then again in the evening for Bible study."

"It would be interesting if we could hear from him, but I'm sure he's long gone by now," Debbie said.

"He is. He retired around the time of the train robbery. It was a bittersweet event for my grandmother. I understand Pastor Darrel was like family. I might be able to track down his son or grandson in my address book. Let me do some digging and get back to you."

A flash of blue outside the parlor door arrested Debbie's attention. Was someone listening in on their conversation? Before she could try to figure it out, Richard entered the room with a silver tray of teacups and a steaming teapot. "Tea. As you requested, Aunt."

Debbie shut the record book and slid it beneath another photo album.

Beatrice motioned her nephew to the coffee table and moved the photos to make space for his tray. "Ah, good of you to make yourself useful. Sit down, Richard. Do tell the women your recent news. They are close friends of mine and will certainly celebrate with you."

Debbie tensed as he settled next to her on the couch.

He didn't seem to notice her discomfort. "I'm planning to volunteer with the local fire department."

"That's not all," Beatrice added. "Richard is also working on his EMT license. We need good ambulance drivers in this community. Men who will stay in a small town. I couldn't be prouder of my nephew."

He grunted again, reminiscent of a wild Viking with that rugged beard and long, curly hair. Debbie murmured tepid congratulations, as did Janet. At least Beatrice was happy with her nephew's progress. And at least he was making progress.

Debbie spent the next several minutes examining photographs with Beatrice, Richard, and Janet. Richard appeared to thaw as he joked with Beatrice over the possibility of uncovering more items in her attic. Debbie, however, couldn't laugh. Instead, she slowly inched away from Richard, unable to forget how he'd threatened her with a lawsuit.

"Only if you promise to clean it out," Beatrice retorted playfully, clearly oblivious to Debbie's discomfort. Janet, however, flashed Debbie a sympathetic smile.

Richard chuckled as he stroked his beard. "I will. But honestly, Aunt Beatrice, you need updates on the house to keep it in shape. You could reopen Morrow House as a bed-and-breakfast if we haul out the junk. Say the word, and I'll remove the boxes we've gone through this week."

"We'll see. First, I want to get my family's memoirs published. Then we'll talk about opening an inn."

Debbie shared a look with Janet. Had they misread Richard's intent? Perhaps he really was trying to help Beatrice. Judging from the amount of history stored in haphazard boxes upstairs, Beatrice needed someone to do the heavy lifting. The banter continued while Debbie's thoughts returned to the ledger she'd hidden from Richard's view.

If Myrtle was the mysterious thief on the train, what had happened to her? And what happened to the train loot?

When Debbie glanced through the large bay window overlooking the yard, she saw Vicky walking around, seemingly surveying the brown grass and muddy garden. What was the ghostwriter up to? Was she merely coming up with the best way to portray the property in the Morrow memoirs—or did she have another reason to appraise the grounds?

The image of Vicky frozen in the upstairs bedroom, her hand brushing her pocket, filled Debbie with new misgivings. Jewelry belonging to Beatrice had disappeared, both from her home and Debbie's. Whoever had taken it must have had access to both houses.

Beatrice might trust her family and friends, but should Debbie do the same?

CHAPTER FIFTEEN

Dennison, Ohio
January 11, 1942

The women of Morrow House begged Myrtle to join them for an evening Bible study. She politely demurred until Esmé shushed the women and told them to leave Myrtle alone.

But as the women piled into two cars, she snatched her overcoat and joined them, despite her resolution not to return to the church. The house of worship did strange things to her. It invited unfamiliar thoughts, dragging her from her current course of action. She ought to rest and go over every detail of Gavin's plan and prepare herself for the inevitable disaster. On the other hand, she couldn't stop her fingers from shaking. Perhaps a distraction might help her focus better.

The church was well lit at night, its welcoming glow pushing back the darkness of the evening. She entered the brick building, mindful of Esmé at her side. Tonight would be Myrtle's last night in Dennison. In a little more than twenty-four hours, she would be far away—wherever Gavin decreed—and the idea of being alone with him again made her skin crawl.

There was safety to be found inside the Morrow House. Grace. Compassion. Generosity. Hospitality. Friendship too, if she had the inclination to stay. Esmé's youngest daughter, Louise, sidled up to Myrtle while Pastor Darrel led the Bible study. He read from 1 Corinthians, chapter six. Some of it blurred past her, but one passage made the hair on the back of her neck rise to attention.

"'Nor thieves, nor covetous, nor drunkards, nor revilers, nor extortioners, shall inherit the kingdom of God.'" Pastor Darrel paused dramatically, his gaze sweeping across those gathered and landing on Myrtle. "'And such were some of you: but ye are washed, but ye are sanctified, but ye are justified in the name of the Lord Jesus, and by the Spirit of our God.'"

She blinked rapidly, her throat tightening as she touched the pearls around her neck. The heavy strand grounded her, comforted her, as memories of her mother reading from the Corinthians passage filled her mind.

But her husband's voice, taunting and cruel, also toyed with her. "You were rich, Mimi. You don't know how to live any other way. You had the best of everything. Ballet. Horseback riding. Fencing. Language lessons. There wasn't anything your devoted daddy wouldn't do for his precious girl to see her get ahead in life. If you want the same privileged lifestyle, darling, you're going to have to put your skills to good use. All of them."

Her mother would be so ashamed if she knew the extent of Myrtle's sins. Like so many others, her family had lost everything during the Great Depression. She had married Arnold, hoping to restore the family's wealth. Never once had she guessed the unsavory methods her husband had used to claw his way to the top. Never had she imagined the well-dressed man at her side was a mobster.

But then again, she had ignored the subtle warning signs. And she had ignored her mother's pleas not to marry such an arrogant man. He had lavished gifts and attention on her, and she'd thought she was doing what was best for her family. She had willfully stepped into a cage of his making and shut the door behind herself.

When the service ended, Myrtle offered a wobbly smile to the sweet Louise, who had sat so quietly beside her. Would Walter approve of his mother attending church? She knew he would, and she found that she didn't want to leave, even though Pastor Darrel's words pierced her to the core.

From her peripheral vision, she caught the pastor watching her fumble for her purse and the threadbare handkerchief hiding inside.

"I'm glad you came back, Mrs. Cooper," he said when he approached her. "I'm assuming that was your husband I saw getting off the train the other day? Perhaps he will come to service next Sunday?"

She startled at his question, to say nothing of the idea of Gavin as her husband. "No, he's—he's not the sort to come to church."

Darrel appeared so concerned, she nearly squirmed in her haste to escape his questions. He nodded slowly, his keen eyes seemingly missing nothing. "I'm glad you're here. God has a way of bringing us to Him when we need Him the most."

As she grabbed her coat from the entrance while Esmé and the other women visited quietly, she couldn't help pondering his innocent statement. Was God trying to reach her? Did He even see her? The Black Cat, master thief?

She pushed the heavy wooden door open and stepped out into the darkness and the cold, too troubled to seek an answer to that pressing question.

January 12, 1942

Jack adjusted his leather gloves and pulled the brim of his fedora lower. No one would recognize him, as he didn't know a single soul in Dennison, but he had years of caution ingrained into his very fiber.

"Next stop, Dennison," the conductor announced as he walked the train aisle.

The trip from Washington, DC had been a long one, with plenty of stops and hair-raising transfers. The idea of traveling with only one agent still had him on edge. He much preferred his entire team at his side, even if they were incognito.

But the boss had been firm. Larry Chapman, the one agent allowed him, sat in the more affordable seating, while Jack lounged in first class. His superior had assured him that they had taken every precaution, but there was no telling what trouble he might encounter on his own.

Jack shifted on the plush seat, his gaze scanning the occupants. Might one of the men sitting in this car with him be the buyer Renee had warned him about? Or was the buyer already in Dennison, waiting for him?

Jack had no choice but to trust Renee's intel. If all went well, Ricky would finally travel out of DC. A rare feat, fitting for the history books.

He overheard the two women behind him talking about the inclement weather. One woman clucked her tongue. "I didn't know they expect a blizzard tomorrow. I would never have risked traveling if I had."

The other woman replied in a strident voice, "At least be thankful we're missing it by a day. Finally, we'll get to see the family again. It's been far too long. I can hardly wait to see all my grandchildren..."

Jack tuned out the rest of the conversation, praying the blizzard would somehow work in his favor.

His anxiety ratcheted up when he heard the hiss of the engine and the wheels screeching to a halt as the train eased up next to the platform. A few of the other men in the car were hidden behind newspapers, and he longed to get a good look at their faces.

Jack stood and stretched his arms, relieving the tension and weary muscles as the other passengers did, and then he left his seat for a brief reprieve, arguing with himself that it would appear more suspicious if he stayed put. It felt good to walk after the long trip.

Might he find a treat of some kind inside the station? A newsstand, perhaps? Despite the hot meal earlier and plenty of coffee, he wouldn't mind an extra bite to eat. He got off the train and found himself pressed on all sides by passengers and their families and friends. The station was nice and looked well maintained.

"Do you have any baggage needing tending, sir?" asked a teenager in the crisp uniform of a porter.

"No, thank you. My luggage will remain in the storage car."

The youth gave him a friendly grin. "If you need anything, ask for Harry, sir. I'll help you right away."

"Actually, Harry, I'd appreciate if you could give me some information. Have you noticed any men traveling in a group? Perhaps well-dressed, arriving today or yesterday?"

Harry chuckled. "Yes, sir. Lots of young men travel together these days. Many well dressed, in sharp-looking uniforms. I think you'll have your work cut out for you finding your friends."

Jack couldn't help laughing at the teenager's humor. He found the arrivals-departures board and studied the train schedules. Then he walked around outside for a few minutes.

The snow fell in thick swirls, with heavy flakes sure to harden into ice. It was cold, which was good for Ricky. Better icy temperatures than the moist heat of a southern state.

Jack headed inside the station, stamping his freshly shined shoes at the entrance and taking in the surprisingly long line at the ticket booth. As he waited to purchase a paper from the stand, he scanned the crowd. No unusual characters. No surly men. No shifty eyes or darting glances. Everyone seemed innocent, including the young men who were enlisting, based on the teary farewells from loved ones.

He shelled out a few coins for the paper and skimmed the headlines. THE BATTLE FOR THE NETHERLANDS BEGINS. Beneath it, in smaller type: WHERE DID THE BLACK CAT GO? The idea of a woman thief was far more intriguing to Jack, even if the war remained all-consuming.

Someone bumped his shoulder, and he dropped the paper.

"I'm so sorry." A woman reached down to pick it up from the polished floor, her dark curls caught beneath a white headscarf. She wore a long overcoat and pants. Now that was unusual. Sure, a glamorous celebrity had made menswear fashionable for women, but it was hardly a common sight. This woman, however, sported no glamor or rebellious edge. She was plain, with dingy boots and threadbare clothes. Her cheeks and lips were bare of makeup.

"Your paper?" She handed it to him.

"Thank you," he replied. "It's crowded at the station today, despite the weather."

She nodded, her mouth quirked to one side, as she passed him.

He thought nothing more about her after guessing that she was no doubt dressed as she was for farm chores or other manual labor. Instead, his attention was captured by a group of men in business suits. One of them peered over his shoulder as if to measure the exits. To Jack's left, Larry slouched against the wall, yawning for all to see.

With a slight nod, Jack indicated his intent to the other agent before spinning on his heel and walking straight toward the men.

Every nerve screamed inside Myrtle when the swarthy stranger with the fedora and the newspaper pinned beneath his arm hurried away from her. It had taken all her strength not to stare at the headline, which had stubbornly persisted for the past several days. Journalists continued to speculate about where the Black Cat had ventured after fleeing prison. Only a worldwide war was enough to distract from her feat.

Grateful for her large coat that hid the shaking brought on by adrenaline, she stuffed her hands into her oversize pockets, where Pastor Darrel's mittens waited, safe and warm.

Her luggage stood next to the counter. Just a quick visit to see an ailing family member, she had informed the staff here at the station. No one questioned her too much, not with all the volunteers pouring in to help at the canteen. Plenty of pink-cheeked girls wanted to interact with the soldiers as they left Dennison to venture into the great unknown. She wondered if Walter would have a girl by his side when he left for the war in a few months.

If she could, she would visit her boy. But the truth had a way of seeping into her mind, reminding her of all the pressing reasons she couldn't yet. Or maybe cruel fate would separate her from him forever. But if that was the only way she could keep him safe, so be it.

Out of the corner of her eye, she noticed Gavin come into the station. He wore a plain suit and a wool scarf wrapped around his neck, as ragged and country as could be. He hadn't balked at her fashion recommendations when she'd brought the bag of clothes to the hotel. Instead, he stored his elegant suits in an alligator suitcase to travel with Jimmy. Without gold cuff links and starched white shirts, he blended in with the crowd, his hair free of pomade. He appeared almost normal. Handsome, even. But she knew better, and she shuddered for the girls who glanced his way.

The stranger with the newspaper passed Gavin and approached a smartly dressed passenger. With a deep breath, she nodded once at Gavin and picked up her worn carpetbag with its loose handle and another suitcase that held snowshoes. She checked the snowshoe case at the counter and then headed toward the train.

"Miss Cooper, you're wearing pants," a familiar boyish voice cried from behind her. Harry pulled a trolley loaded with luggage and wore his trademark grin.

A smile crossed her lips. She liked Harry. He was a little younger than her son and full of promise and youthful enthusiasm. Perhaps Walter could have been more carefree if not for the life she and his father had dumped him into. "It's cold, Harry. Don't you know a blizzard's coming? Every farm girl pulls out her dungarees when the weather turns wretched."

"I know well enough how wretched it can be. When I finish work, I'll be shoveling the sidewalk at my house." He shuddered.

"An excellent workout for a sturdy kid like you," she teased.

"If you say so. See you when you get back." He waved then hauled the trolley of luggage away from the train and toward the platform where passengers waited.

Smile fading, she returned her attention to the burgundy baggage car with its double sliding doors on each end and precious few windows. During her stay in Dennison, she had learned that the storage cars often carried mail as well as expedited freight, which provided the railroad companies a tremendous profit. Harry had said the items needed to be switched out and delivered as quickly as possible at stops. Luggage and bulky items passengers wanted to transport would fill the remaining space to capacity.

Her choices were few. Sit in the cheapest seat away from the other coach cars, face the soldiers in the dining car that sold them enticing refreshments, or mingle with the first-class businessmen and fancy ladies near the enormous windows, where she would enjoy the marvelous view and stick out like a sore thumb.

Gavin wanted this heist to be discreet. If they played their roles well, they might be able to pull it off with no one getting hurt. The last time her husband had insisted on taking the lead on a job, too many innocents had fallen. To her relief, Gavin had reluctantly agreed with her idea, admitting that it would be easier to fly under the radar if they harmed no one. Then again, he had made her plenty of promises he had broken without a second thought in the heat of the moment.

Please don't let anyone get hurt.

She hadn't prayed in so long, but this one circled around and around in her mind.

A glance at her wristwatch brought the familiar rush of adrenaline, the feeling at once familiar and shameful. It had once excited her, but she was older and wiser now. Heartbreakingly wiser.

About half an hour until departure.

Then the real work would begin.

CHAPTER SIXTEEN

On Wednesday, Debbie called the members of the Easter celebration committee to discuss the missing pearls. No one volunteered information other than Greg, who again vowed to do everything he could to help her.

I'm still horrified that one of our people might have stolen from you, he had texted her shortly before supper.

She felt horrified as well, to be honest. At least her phone was now silent, which felt strange after days of being bombarded with requests about the floats and Easter egg hunt.

She unlocked her phone screen and studied the photograph of the woman with the pearls around her neck then swiped to the photo of Pastor Armstrong. Beatrice had provided many pictures, including several of the church Greg was currently renovating. In the pictures, the building appeared beautifully maintained, a beacon of hope and redemption to all who entered Dennison.

She needed another lead beyond sepia-toned photos. Beatrice's mother, Louise, and Pastor Darrel had passed years before. Who was left to help Debbie track down the elusive wearer of the magnificent South Sea pearls?

As if she'd summoned it with her thought process, a text from Richard appeared.

I'VE HEARD NOTHING FROM YOU ABOUT THE PEARLS. I WASN'T KIDDING WHEN I SAID I WOULD PURSUE FULL LEGAL ACTION. DON'T STEAL FROM MY AUNT, DEBBIE. SHE'S DONE SO MUCH GOOD FOR THE COMMUNITY. IT'S AWFUL FOR YOU TO REPAY HER THIS WAY, EVEN IF IT IS SIMPLY CARELESSNESS ON YOUR PART. I WANT ANSWERS AND I WANT THEM SOON.

She fought the temptation to delete his words and block the insufferable man, but she might need these messages in the future, in case he brought litigation. Yet the menacing tone made her shiver. She already felt sick about the lost pearls.

She could only think of one option to help her find them. Everything hinged on whether the mysterious Myrtle Cooper who left the pearls as payment for her stay at the boardinghouse was also the female thief who got away. If she was, and if Debbie could find out more about Myrtle, maybe she could discover the lost treasure and lure the thief out into the open. Greed often proved a tremendous motivator.

Debbie returned her attention to the photo of the smiling pastor.

Louise and Beatrice had kept in touch with the Armstrong family. Right after he retired, Darrel and his wife had moved to Akron be near their two sons and grandchildren. Beatrice had found one of his grandson's contact information and texted it to Debbie.

Debbie composed a text message to Oliver Armstrong, introducing herself and explaining what she was after. Then she attached the picture of the aged photograph. Praying Oliver would be open to talk to her, she pressed Send.

Needing something to do other than stare at her phone waiting for a response that might not come, she decided to reheat a plate of stir-fry for supper. Her mind drifted back to the image of Vicky studying Beatrice's yard. Was she searching for something on the Morrow property like Richard was? With a former carriage house converted to a garage, a sunken-in icehouse that should likely be condemned, and an old glass conservatory, there remained plenty of hiding places yet to explore—not to mention the huge mansion itself. But how could someone hide a treasure with a house full of women watching?

Then again, why would anyone be foolish enough to rob a train loaded with soldiers?

The microwave beeped, and Debbie pulled out the sizzling dish. When she returned to the coffee table, she saw that her phone was flashing with a new text. Oliver Armstrong.

Ms. Albright, I'm delighted to make your acquaintance. Yes, I remember Beatrice Morrow. Her grandmother and my grandfather were great friends. Why don't you call me? I might be able to answer some of your questions.

She dialed his number immediately.

The call was picked up at once, and an older male voice sounded in her ear. "This is Oliver."

After further introductions and background regarding the photo, pearls, and the note, Oliver readily offered information. "My grandfather used to tell us the most amazing stories about his years of ministry and the men and women who needed comfort. I can't remember names, but he might have written about a Myrtle Cooper in his journal. He kept prayer lists of all the Dennison residents, including their names and the dates he prayed for them. I've got it right beside his Bible in my study. Let me go get it."

Oliver peppered her with questions about Dennison as he walked to his study, and Debbie got the distinct impression he was glad to have someone to talk to. She was happy to answer his questions.

Finally, he said, "I've got it. Now, what was the date again?"

"January 12, 1942," she told him.

"Right. After Pearl Harbor and with the threat of war looming in the Pacific," he murmured, as if to himself. "My grandfather loved to tell us stories of the train station that sent soldiers all over the country. I've got to visit it again one of these days."

"If you do, please stop by and see us. My friend Janet and I recently opened the Whistle Stop Café in the station, and there's also a very interesting museum."

"That sounds wonderful. I'll come this summer." There was a long pause, as if he was scanning the journal. Then he gave a cry of triumph. "Here she is, Debbie. My grandfather prayed over many people, and Myrtle Cooper was one of them. He wrote, 'Myrtle wears a strand of black pearls that doesn't match her rather shabby clothes.' That description matches the woman in the photograph, right? He goes on to say 'She has a son named Walter, who lives in Cleveland. I am afraid for her, though she won't tell me any more about her life. She seems to be running from something or someone.'"

Oliver mumbled under his breath as if he was skimming another entry. Then he said, "My grandfather tried to keep in touch with Myrtle, but she seems to have vanished into thin air. I doubt she's still alive. She was probably in her mid to late thirties, according to my grandfather's description of her, which would make her well over a hundred today. I'm sorry it's not much, but I hope it helps. Perhaps you can find her son or one of his descendants."

"That's a great idea." Debbie put her pencil down and said, "Do you think you could take pictures of those notes and send them to me?"

"I don't know how to do that, but I know my granddaughter could. She stops by here a couple of times a week, and I'll ask her to do it for me."

"Thank you so much," Debbie said. "And I look forward to your visit this summer."

"Just a minute," Oliver said. "Here's something else that might interest you. My grandfather also wrote about a strange man who came to visit Myrtle. He says, 'Maybe a husband? A boyfriend? But whoever he was, he obviously terrifies her.'"

CHAPTER SEVENTEEN

Snow fell in swirls, the flakes bitingly cold. The gathering wind stung Myrtle's cheeks before she ducked inside the coach and found an empty seat close to the baggage car. She sank down, welcoming the fresh powder falling outside. It would make running in snowshoes so much easier.

She drew her coat closer around herself and gazed out the window, her breath clouding the glass as passengers crowded the car.

She felt Gavin's presence, her skin prickling in response. Raising her head, she saw him standing in the doorway. He wore an expression that sent chills up her spine. His mouth quirked as he angled his big frame down the aisle toward her.

She had racked her brain for solutions to the problem at hand, wondering how could she flee from Gavin's grip. She had come up empty. There was no going back now.

He settled next to her and flung an arm around her shoulders. Even the thick wool of his coat couldn't disguise his touch. She shuddered.

"Still cold, darling?" His smirk widened.

She didn't respond, focusing on the wool mittens in her coat pockets. Funny how comforting they had become to her. A gift with nothing demanded in return. A glimpse of humanity amid the chaos of her life.

He removed his arm. "Let's synchronize our watches," he said as he pushed up his frayed plaid cuff to reveal a gold watch.

She did the same, maneuvering her watch hands so that they ticked along with Gavin's. Meanwhile, her gaze darted over the dim interior of the train. To her left and right, a narrow set of windows allowed in the silver light. Doors lay behind and in front of her, and beyond the small glass window of the exit, she spotted the door to the baggage car.

Two exits. But neither of them did her any good.

"It's a full car," she muttered. Was it any use to pray for no violence this time around, or would God scorn her request?

Gavin leaned toward her, the scent of his musky cologne thick and overly sweet. "No one will bother us. Just pretend we're newlyweds. Which will require you to behave as if you actually like me. At the right time, the train will grind to a halt, and we'll move to the baggage car. Jimmy's already making friends with the rest of the passengers, and Sylvester left half an hour ago to head out to the country."

The train would stop outside of Dennison, directly north of where the empty farmhouse lay. Last night, they had parked the getaway car there, leaving the key in the ignition and the tank full of gas. She hoped it would start despite the extreme cold.

Gavin tapped his foot while she folded her arms across her chest and took deep, regular breaths in an attempt to slow her pulse's frenetic pace, mentally picturing the train. She would need to keep the whole layout in mind to pull this off.

A man in a fedora dashed into the car, clutching a briefcase and a rolled-up newspaper. She ducked her head, her chest constricting as she recognized the man she had bumped into inside the station.

A hum of chatter filled the car as excited passengers settled in their seats. The train hissed and the whistle blew loudly, signaling that departure was imminent.

Gavin's smile slipped a notch when he noticed something outside the train. Myrtle followed his line of vision and noted the number of people pressing forward to enter the train.

"We've got a crowd with us. You'll have to move fast," he whispered in her ear.

She fingered the rough wool of the mitten in her pocket. "Don't worry about me. Worry about the engineer stopping, or you and I might break our necks jumping from a speeding train."

For once, Gavin didn't offer her his usual dismissive replies, and worry settled deeper as the train jolted forward. Minutes ticked past as the train left Dennison. The buildings grew smaller and smaller behind them, and before long, she saw snow-covered farmland flashing past. Telephone poles blurred, along with the hay bales dotting the landscape. Snow fell harder and faster, proving the rumors of a wicked storm were true.

So many things could go wrong. She and Gavin might not even make it to the baggage car before they were caught. Someone could glance out the window at the wrong time and witness two figures leaving the train and sprinting across the fields. Or they could reach the farm and find driving impossible due to the snowdrifts and the lack of visibility. She found herself *hoping that something would happen to keep Sylvester from parking the car on the tracks. Maybe she wouldn't have to do this after all.*

But the warning whistle shrieked, and the train ground to a halt several miles outside of Dennison. It was time. She rose from her seat.

"Let's hope Jimmy can act," she muttered as Gavin stood at her side. Perhaps no one would think twice about their movements.

Without another word, they slipped out of their seats, and Gavin opened the small door to the baggage car. Thankfully, it was unlocked, as it had been when she'd checked before boarding. No one followed them or called out to them.

Swathed in shadows and much colder than the rest of the train, the baggage car was devoid of life. She ignored the temperature drop and followed Gavin past rows of luggage and wooden crates. Two small windows on the left wall allowed the twilight reflecting off the snow to light their way.

Gavin shifted crates, examining them for something while his breath billowed white with each exhale. He hadn't told her what he was trying to find, so she couldn't help. While he searched, she located her suitcase that contained the two sets of snowshoes. The snowshoes were made of wicker, wrapped in treated sinew, and light as a feather. Gavin had purchased them from a pawnshop somewhere in Chicago.

With a hiss of triumph, Gavin produced a small crowbar from his coat and pointed to a box about two feet high. It was large. Larger than she had expected. It was stamped WASHINGTON, DC.

Washington? Was I right? Are we stealing something from the government?

"Aren't you going to tell me what's inside the crate?" she demanded. "I think I deserve to know."

"You'll see soon enough." Despite his even tone, his hands shook as he jammed the crowbar into the gap between the lid and the side of the crate. With a loud creak of nails prying loose, it opened. He pushed aside the lid, letting it clatter to the floor. Shredded newspaper and packing paper covered the contents like a bird's nest.

With both hands, he dug into the packing, a bright grin flashing across his face when he pulled out a—

Her breath caught as confusion washed over her.

A large manila envelope? Several envelopes, in fact. He reached into his inner coat pocket and withdrew a pocketknife. Then he carefully slit one of the sealed envelopes.

"Don't let me down, Renee. Tell me you packed the goods," he whispered. Myrtle mentally filed the name. He had uttered it before on his phone call at the diner.

"There we are." He carefully slid out an aged sheet, with the writing so faded it was barely legible. The elegant scrawl put her penmanship to shame. "These envelopes are stuffed with the sweetest prizes. Did you know that the Magna Carta, on loan from Britain for the world's fair in 1939 and left here because of the German invasions, has been in the Library of Congress all this time? My contact gave me a list of fine art and other items being shipped out to undisclosed locations all over the United States. Over five thousand boxes, all loaded with the most priceless artifacts you ever saw."

"We're stealing from the Library of Congress?" She had to keep a tight rein on her voice to avoid screaming. "And you have a buyer?"

"With cultural heritage treasures like this? I could place them on the black market and demand anything, even ransom from our government. To say nothing of certain foreign governments who are paying me to cause this bit of mischief in the first place." Gavin's triumphant tone made her toes curl. "Do you get it now? You see how important this is to our future? We'll be rich, Mimi. The richest couple in all of America. Why settle for Mexico? Let's head to Morocco and live in a palace. Strap on those snowshoes. We're going to run into a brilliant future."

Yes, the future was at stake. But not merely hers and Gavin's. Her son's future as well. And the future of every mother's son in the United States. In a matter of months, Walter would enlist in the army and likely fight the very enemies who were funding this heist.

Pastor Darrel's voice whispered encouragement to her. You can change.

But how could she say no to such powerful men? Then again, how could she betray her country and her son? She tugged on the document that Gavin had gloated over, drawing it just enough out of the envelope that she could see what it was.

A cold ball of horror settled in her stomach. Dear God, no.

CHAPTER EIGHTEEN

Work on a Thursday was as busy as ever. After the breakfast crowd left, Debbie slid into a freshly cleaned booth while Paulette poured more coffee for a lingering couple. Janet followed Debbie, scooting in across the table with a cup of coffee for each of them.

Debbie didn't mind the extra jolt of caffeine. She was exhausted between running the café, trying to locate Beatrice's mystery woman and the lost pearls, and organizing the Easter celebration.

Janet eyed her over the rim of her mug as she sipped her coffee. "You need a vacation," she said.

"You do too," Debbie answered, keeping her tone light.

"No, I mean it, Debbie. You can't go on saying yes to everything. You're going to burn out at this rate."

"You're right. I've truly learned my lesson. But I do have to push through and finish my commitments." Debbie fingered the handle of her coffee cup. Her ready acquiescence, however, didn't sound entirely convincing, even to her ears.

Janet shook her head. "No one has come forward about the missing pearls yet, have they?"

"Not a single person. What I really need to do is solve the riddle of Beatrice's mysterious boardinghouse guest and find out once and for all whether or not she has any ties to the train robbery.

Unfortunately, I can't find a single newspaper article detailing what was taken in the heist."

She was about to say more when her phone rang. She slid it out of her back pocket and swiped the screen.

"Is this Debbie Albright?" asked a female voice. "This is Julie Cooper, returning your call." Some late-night digging had revealed that Myrtle Cooper's son, Walter, had passed away, but he'd had a daughter named Julie. Debbie had left her a voice message early that morning.

"Thank you so much for calling me back," Debbie said. Out of the corner of her eye, she saw the familiar and welcome form of Harry Franklin entering the café with his faithful dog, Crosby.

Unfortunately, another familiar figure followed right behind them, her hair perfectly curled and her outfit as sparkly as usual. Gloria.

Harry waved when he saw Debbie. Gloria, however, wore a stony expression.

Debbie held up a finger to let them know she'd be with them in a moment and focused on her call. Julie, a high school history teacher, had never met her grandmother.

"You mean you never got a phone call or visit?" Debbie asked. Her grandparents had been such a crucial and loving part of her own childhood that she couldn't imagine growing up without them.

"Not one," Julie answered. "According to my father, the last time he talked to her, he was seventeen. The only communication he had from her after that was four coded messages she placed in the classified section of the *Plain Dealer*. And then after a couple or three months, the messages simply stopped, which I have to assume meant that she passed away. My father came to the same conclusion, and it broke his heart."

Debbie's skin prickled as she pressed her phone against her ear. "Why would she do something so—so—"

"Clandestine?" Julie supplied. "I think she was afraid. I've kept the messages, if you'd like to see them. Unfortunately, Dad and I couldn't make heads or tails of them. She knew my father loved history. Two of the messages were passages from classic poems."

Gloria inched closer, tapping her watch as if to tell Debbie to hurry the conversation.

"I'll take care of Gloria and Harry," Janet murmured, but at that moment, Paulette came through the door and grabbed her apron. Janet sank back into the booth to nurse her coffee.

"I would like to see the messages, if that's all right with you," Debbie said, lowering her voice so no one other than Janet would hear.

"Sure. Maybe you can come up with some better answers than I've been able to. It's strange, really. Grandma sent Dad four messages, and that's it. He never could figure out what she was trying to tell him."

"I'm so sorry," Debbie murmured.

"Thank you. I'm grateful I had a great dad who loved his family. Honestly, my grandmother was a complicated woman with lots of secrets. My father grieved when he realized the messages had stopped. But he said that if she was still alive, she must have been in some kind of trouble—that his father had been a dangerous man with bad friends. He feared that, somehow, those friends got to her." The background noise on Julie's end of the line increased. "Debbie, my break is over, and I have a class coming in now. Will you keep me posted if you figure anything out?"

"Of course. And thanks for being willing to talk to me."

"Sure thing. If I think of anything else, I'll be in touch." The call ended.

Debbie's pulse picked up as she mulled over the conversation. She knew she had a café to run, but it was difficult to concentrate.

"Debbie!" Harry called out as he leaned on his cane. "Why the frown? Is everything all right?"

She chuckled and motioned him over to the booth. "Come and join Janet and me for coffee."

Crosby trotted alongside Harry, plopping down at his owner's feet when Harry settled beside Debbie. Crosby was a minor celebrity in town because he was related to a famous World War I dog named Bing, who had a fascinating history linked to the depot.

"It's too late in the day for coffee for me. I'm here for the doughnuts," Harry said with a wink.

Janet's eyes were wide as her glance slid to Debbie's phone. Debbie guessed her friend was dying to know about the phone conversation. Poor Janet would just have to wait a bit longer.

"Harry, as a porter, you encountered a lot of people during the war. Did you ever meet a woman who wore a necklace of black pearls? It's not much to go on, I know. But if I showed you a photograph, I thought perhaps you could help me track down more information about her."

"Show me," he said with a twinkle in his brown eyes. "You know I love to help you on your historical quests."

It was true. He delighted in teasing her and Janet about digging up Dennison's rich history and finding plenty of trouble mixed in with the stories. But she suspected he enjoyed the mysteries as much as she did. She quickly found the photo on her phone and showed it to him.

He took the phone, squinting at the picture and then enlarging it to see the detail better, humming in thought.

She watched him closely, afraid to speak for fear of distracting him from a memory.

At last, he announced, "I *do* remember this lady. Her name was Myrtle Cooper. She worked at the station for maybe a couple of weeks one winter, taking in everything with those enormous eyes of hers. She was so quiet compared to the others, but a gracious woman. Midthirties, or even forty, I suspect. When she arrived, Pastor Darrel gave her a ride to the Morrow House and even helped her find work at the station. Not too long after, she said she had to go visit family, and we never saw her again. I asked Pastor Darrel about her, but he'd get all strange and not tell me a word. I bet you anything he knew something. But if you ask me, she was in some kind of danger."

"Why do you say that?" Janet asked as she leaned forward, resting her elbows on the table.

He frowned. "Her face was familiar. I noticed her right away. Oh, she was as poor as a church mouse, except for that necklace, perhaps. So she was nobody famous, like a movie star. But she reminded me of someone. I never figured out who. And then a man came to town, dressed all fancy and rich with gold cuff links. Maybe he thought no one was listening to his conversation, but he called her Mimi. Pastor Darrel heard the same as I did."

"Mimi," Debbie repeated. "That *is* interesting. No one has mentioned that name to me."

She'd have to find out more about that tidbit of information. Maybe Julie could help.

Harry's expression sobered as he stroked Crosby's head. "Want to know something else? One of my good friends at the time served as a waitress at the local diner, and she overhead the man make a phone call. He terrified her. Yelled at her, if I remember correctly, for walking too close to the phone while he was talking. Poor kid. That bad memory stuck with her. She said he was talking to someone in Washington, DC."

"I wonder why someone would call Washington. Family, perhaps?" Janet asked. Her coffee appeared forgotten.

"My friend said she heard the stranger joke about a library and all the boring books inside it."

Debbie rubbed her chin. She felt goose bumps flare to life along her arms and the back of her neck. The feeling that something wasn't quite right swamped her. She had experienced the same sensation at the library when searching for articles regarding the train robbery—a robbery that had barely scratched national news.

"Do you remember the train robbery on January 12, 1942?" she asked Harry.

He nodded, his expression suddenly pained. "I do. It happened during a terrible snowstorm. Not quite the blizzard the people on the radio promised us, but it was an awful night all the same. The power went out for some, plunging them into dangerous temperatures, and with little light, it was hard to see in some parts of town.

That was the night I saw Myrtle Cooper for the last time. It was her train out of town that was robbed."

"Wow," Janet murmured.

Debbie glanced around the room to make sure all was well. Gloria sat at a booth across the room, drinking tea and eating a giant cinnamon bun. Otherwise, it was quiet.

She returned her attention to Harry. "Why do you think the major newspapers didn't cover the story?"

He arched a grizzled eyebrow. "They didn't?"

"Not that I found. Only a few local papers and Cincinnati mentioned it."

He blew out a loud breath. "We were headed into a war. Maybe the threat of fighting overseas was considered more newsworthy than a train heist in small-town Dennison? Everyone was worried about the future and the possibility of the Germans invading."

"What did Pastor Darrel think happened to Myrtle?"

Harry's expression fell as he nudged the phone back to Debbie. "Pastor Darrel was a fine man. He took confidentiality very seriously. Once he locked up a secret, nobody could pry it out of him. But he told me he thought Myrtle was in trouble when I asked if he had heard anything from her. That's all he'd say about it though."

A more disturbing thought took hold as Debbie shifted on the bench, suddenly uncomfortable. Had Myrtle—or was it Mimi?—lied to everyone, including a beloved pastor? Had she been involved in the train robbery on January 12, 1942?

CHAPTER NINETEEN

January 12, 1942

Jack sat in one of the modest passenger cars. It wasn't as flashy as first class, but still plenty respectable. Coffee was about to be served, or tea, or something else he had vaguely agreed to—when the train shuddered to a halt.

He unfolded his leg from the relaxed pose of a business traveler and sat up straight. The paper lay on the seat beside him. He scanned the crowded seats buzzing with soldiers and other passengers rising to their feet. One couple left the car altogether. He only got a glimpse of their backs as they disappeared through the door.

Along with everyone else in the car, he staggered to his feet and peered out into the swirling gusts to see what might have caused the train to halt without warning.

"Are we going back because of the blizzard?" a frail older woman asked as she pushed her spectacles up the bridge of her nose. Her fur hat and coat gleamed in the gray light of the window.

"No, dear," her husband, a bald, portly man, replied. "It's likely some malfunction with the engine."

"Or a herd of cattle blocking the tracks and road." A redheaded man, wearing a pinstripe suit, grinned mischievously.

Jack had spoken with the young man at the station, wondering if this was his target. As it turned out, the freckled youth was studying to be a lawyer, and he was returning to school after visiting sick relatives.

The woman shot the younger man a baleful glare. "Surely no one would be so careless as to let their cattle loose near a railroad, especially in this weather. I can't imagine having to be out there in the cold. Do you think they'll make us walk back to Dennison, Monty? I simply couldn't bear even a minute in the cold."

Monty grimaced, equally displeased by the idea.

"We stay put," the soon-to-be lawyer reassured them, flashing yet another crooked grin. "We're warm and cozy in our car. Although I might like to stretch my legs and go to the dining car to see if I can find out what happened."

"I'll join you," Jack said.

He followed the young man into the crowded dining car, where white-clad tables were arranged near the windows. A waiter was bussing a table as Jack stepped into the car.

"Is there anything you can tell us about why the train has stopped?" Jack asked, looking out the window to the left. Snow continued to fall in huge, fluffy flakes. Beyond that, a line of trees and farmland was as serene as could be. An idyllic scene if one were inclined to enjoy the ride. He didn't feel like enjoying much of anything until his mission was done though.

"Yes, sir," the waiter replied easily. "I guess a car has stalled on the tracks."

The lawyer plunked himself down at the table, his features in bored lines. "How exciting. Could we have something hot to drink? Tea? Coffee? Hot chocolate if you have it?" He turned to Jack and gestured to a chair beside him. "If you care to join me."

"No thanks." Jack frowned as the young man pulled a squished sandwich from his coat pocket, unwrapped it, and took a huge bite. Must be a struggling student.

He reengaged the server. "A stall? Now?"

The young man shrugged one shoulder. "It's rare, but then again, the weather isn't too nice right now."

As much as Jack wanted answers, he realized the server had probably told him all he knew. He moved closer to the end of the car, ignoring the other passengers sitting at the tables, murmuring their dismay. Kids volunteering for overseas military service. Businessmen. Women with children.

Suddenly their vague chatter burst into a cacophony of alarm.

He whirled around to see the young law student clutching his throat.

"He's choking! Please, someone help him!" a woman screamed.

Jack rushed toward the man, who had slid to the ground with a gurgle, but someone else—an older man with a waxed mustache—knelt beside him.

"Please get away, everyone. He needs air. Hold on, son. I'm going to—" The older man wrapped his arm around the youth's middle for support. He pounded the young man's back, as if to jar something loose.

Dismay filled Jack as he stared at the scene. Everyone gaped at the student and the volunteer, who raised the sprawled man up to a sitting position to breathe easier.

A stalled train. A man choking and causing a distraction. The occupants crowded closer, shouting out instructions or encouragement.

Before he'd even processed his conclusion and made the conscious decision to do something about it, Jack was jogging to the end of the car, his pulse throbbing to a steady beat. What were the odds of a car blocking the tracks and a choking incident, all at once?

"Sir? I don't think you want to go that way," the waiter called out, but Jack had reached the door of the dining car. He yanked it open as flakes of snow bit into his skin. How could he have been so foolish? He didn't have a moment to warn Larry, who was taking his turn in first class on this leg of the journey.

Was he too late?

No. No, this can't be happening.

Myrtle barely felt Gavin yank the envelope out of her hands. He glared at her as he clutched it against his broad chest. Had she uttered what she was thinking out loud?

"Mimi, I'm tellin' you right now, you'd better get that look off your face. Put those snowshoes on. We have to go." He held on to the precious document while

her brain sluggishly tried to catch up with a world that was suddenly moving too quickly. Carefully, he slid the additional, smaller envelopes into the large package. Knowing what was in one envelope, she was terrified of the contents of the others.

Stupidly, she could only stare at him.

"I'll take your son from you if you don't move. Now!" he snarled at her, his voice more predatory animal than human.

She didn't doubt him for a second. Gavin would take Walter, and her son would never be free again. Gavin Schroeder broke plenty of promises, but he never made idle threats. A faint prayer rose within her, begging for some way out of this awful mess. Would God hear her cry? Or had He turned His back on her forever?

"I'm going. I'm just surprised," she finally rasped. "Quite a haul you have there. I knew it would be big, but I never guessed it would be this big."

His sharp eyes flashed at her answer. The thin sheen of sweat on his brow suggested that he felt as affected as she did. Gulping, she tore her attention away from the packet pinned beneath his arm, the action somehow obscenely careless for the treasure he held.

Breathe, Myrtle. It's a simple heist, easier than a lot of others you've pulled off.

But was it truly? Yes, it had been simple. Almost too simple. Which made her feel even more uneasy, with the fine hair rising on the back of her neck.

A faint vibration rippled through the train car, as if someone had opened or closed a door. The reminder that someone could walk in on them at any second jolted her into action. She grabbed the snowshoes from the bag and offered Gavin the larger pair.

He watched her, his eyes narrowing. "You first, darling," he said between clenched teeth.

"We've got a good quarter of a mile to go to reach the farmhouse," she said in a low voice. "We need to get moving."

She needed him to believe she was his ally rather than a threat. Glancing around the small space, she spied a large wooden crate used for transport. She perched on it to put on her snowshoes.

Her fingers refused to work as she loosened the leather ties. Planting one boot on the left shoe, she managed to tie the strings and secure her foot. Then the other. While she tightened the laces of the snowshoes, Gavin moved toward another box, the envelope still trapped beneath his arm.

"What are you doing?" she asked.

"I want it to appear like a regular robbery. I'm going to steal some other items to throw them off the scent."

"No, Gavin. There's only so much we can carry without it slowing us down. We don't have much time. You need to get your snowshoes on."

He grunted and then agreed with a huff, offering her the envelope and then apparently changing his mind at the last minute. Her breath caught in her chest as he shoved it under his arm and sat down to get his feet strapped to the snowshoes.

"When we get to the car, I've decided we won't wait for the boys," he said. "Sylvester and Jimmy will have to figure things out on their own, but they'll work it out. You and I will drive ahead. We've got to get out of this state as soon as possible."

Myrtle couldn't hide her dismay. "You're leaving them behind?"

He pressed his lips into a tight, white line. "It'll mean bigger cuts for you and me if I do. Didn't I promise Arnold that I would take care of you and the boy?"

He would eventually abandon her too. Maybe even set her up to take the fall should the police get too close. And they would swarm after the two of them, guaranteed.

All at once, her life flashed before her eyes. Choices chased each other in her mind, lightning fast, offering nothing but danger. She thought about her options. When they opened the baggage car door, she could *start running—away from the farm and away from Gavin. As long as he didn't have a gun in the depths of his bulky coat, she might be able to get away. She could run with nothing but her life. Just run.*

She would have to pump her legs faster than she ever had, her back presenting a perfect target.

Gavin finished tying his snowshoes and looked up at her. "I know you better than you know yourself, Mimi," he said slowly. "Don't think you can run from me. Stay put right where you are, like the good little girl you've always been."

Resentment filled her, sharp and acidic, but she curbed her tongue before she said something she truly regretted. "I've never left you yet, Gavin."

But as Gavin rose, with his hand outstretched for hers, the door to the baggage car flew open and a grim-faced man blocked their escape.

"Stop! Don't move a muscle!"

Jack stared at the occupants of the storage car. The woman who had run into him inside the station stared back at him with enormous eyes, her feet encased in snowshoes.

But he didn't have time to question her presence. The big man with her whirled around with an angry roar, reached into his coat pocket—

No Wild West theatrics, Lund. *Victor's voice echoed in his mind.*

Jack hurled himself to the side of the car, narrowly avoiding the wrench the bear of a man threw his way.

Jack pushed up from the ground, his pulse hammering in his throat. "I said stop. I'm not letting you leave the train with that package."

To his shock, the woman leaped toward the man and snatched the envelope from beneath his arm.

The big man snarled at her. "Get the door!"

The woman rushed to oblige, grasping the metal handle and hauling at it with all her might, grunting as she strained. She balanced surprisingly well on snowshoes. She glanced over her shoulder, her harried gaze colliding with Jack's for a fraction of a second.

Jack lunged forward, his body colliding with the man's. They rolled on the dirty floor of the storage car, banging into crates, fists and knees flying furiously. He could only take down one of them at a time, and if he couldn't subdue this man, the woman would escape with the package. He heard her groans of frustration. It seemed the train door didn't want to comply.

The snarling man headbutted him, and stars filled his vision as he gasped for air. Shaking his head to clear it, he plunged forward, his fists flying yet again. A shaft of light flooded the room, and a gust of cold air swirled around him, but he didn't let up.

The man howled and collapsed as Jack landed a right hook on his whiskered jaw.

Jack reached for a pair of handcuffs in his coat pocket. "You want some more? Or are you done?"

"No, no," the big man wheezed as he cradled his jaw. "I surrender."

"Good choice. You can hardly stand up in those shoes, much less escape."

To Jack's surprise, the man laughed, although not without a current of anger as he held out his wrists. His hard gaze flickered to the storage door, now open to the elements. "Maybe not. But she sure can."

With a sinking feeling, Jack allowed his gaze to travel in the same direction, to the blinding white swirling outside—and the small figure racing across the fields as if her life depended upon it.

CHAPTER TWENTY

Right before Thursday evening's committee meeting, Debbie glanced at her coffee table, which resembled the table of any general about to begin battle at dawn. Brochures, papers, and pens were laid out across the surface. Her teacup no longer steamed, the brew long since chilled. A half-eaten peanut butter sandwich waited, forgotten, with a bowl of salad that had gone soggy. At least she was trying to eat healthy. She scooped the food out of the room and into the kitchen.

One of the members of the committee had designed pastel-colored brochures and posters for the upcoming festival. The posters should have been created weeks before, but that was another matter entirely. It had taken long enough to agree on the theme.

The doorbell rang.

Rose and Agatha stood outside Debbie's house, their expressions glum though they were planning a festival. Every committee member had been invited, but the volunteers had begun to give excuses as to why they couldn't be more involved ever since Debbie had questioned them about the pearls.

She had thought offering to host the meeting at her home again would show that she did trust them—and perhaps she might catch someone snooping and get a new lead. But most of the committee members had begged off. Apparently, no one wished to open themselves up to a second round of suspicion.

Janet parked in the driveway and climbed out of her car. "Just the four of us?" she called.

"I think so," Debbie said as she held the door open for her friend. Rose and Agatha had already entered the house. "Maybe a smaller meeting will be easier?"

"No Greg?" Janet asked under her breath as she kicked off one sneaker and then the next.

"No," Debbie said. "He's hoping to get the supplies for the committee's float tonight with his boys—if he gets a free moment."

A sliver of guilt pricked her conscience at the mention of his name, but not once had Greg made her feel bad about putting off a dinner date. She didn't think he had any more time for a leisurely dinner right now than she did.

In the living room, the women settled into their seats and Debbie called the meeting to order.

"We still don't have anyone lined up to wear the bunny suit," Agatha said as she folded her arms across her chest, her scowl deepening.

Debbie massaged her temples. That suit was going to be the death of her. It lay inside her car, the cardboard box taking up a significant portion of her back seat. Hopefully, the night wouldn't bring more conflict surrounding it or any other topic that had become a sore subject for the committee.

Rose threw up her hands, and Debbie saw a flicker of a grin on her face. "Fine, I'll do it. My grandkids will think it's cool, especially if I get to throw out candy. Are you satisfied, Agatha? I'm doing it for you and for the kids."

Agatha raised her eyebrows, but a slow smile stretched across her face. "Very satisfied. And actually a little impressed."

"But I'm going to ask you to wear a green hat and something orange." Rose waggled her finger at her. "If I have to be a bunny, you have to be a carrot."

To Debbie's surprise, Agatha laughed heartily. "Deal."

Maybe they would survive this meeting after all.

The doorbell rang again, and Debbie's chest tightened. Janet answered it, and Gloria sauntered into the room.

The blond woman dropped her suede satchel onto the couch and plunked down beside it. "It appears I missed a good time. I heard laughter."

Rose smiled, her eyes sparkling. "I'm going to wear the bunny suit. Agatha will dress up like a carrot to be a good sport."

"We've got the candy purchased," Janet added. "And the posters are done, so the next step is for everyone to hang them up in local businesses."

"I wouldn't mind trying on the suit," Rose said as she picked up a poster. "I hope I can fit into it. Gloria is pretty small compared to me."

Gloria waved a dismissive hand. "You'll be fine, Rose. I'm sure it will fit beautifully, and the kids will be so pleased."

"I'll go get it," Debbie murmured, suddenly remembering she had intended to bring the box inside the house but had completely forgotten. Again. Janet was right. After she finished her current commitments, she needed to take a break. With all the distractions, she could hardly keep anything straight these days.

She slipped on her flats and stepped out into the brisk spring air, which felt cool and damp. She opened her car door—which she rarely locked, since there wasn't much of value inside—and pulled the box toward herself. It was lighter than she'd expected, and the only thing visible through the window on the top was the bottom of the box.

The hideous blue bunny suit was gone.

When Debbie told the women the news, they all gasped.

"You're kidding, aren't you?" Gloria demanded as she crossed one leg over the other. "You'd better be kidding."

"I wish I was." Debbie looked at the empty box, which she'd brought inside and set on the coffee table. "I don't understand it. The box hasn't left my car since you brought it to the café."

Shaking her head, Gloria lifted one of the loose flaps with her manicured finger. "This is dreadful. I rent this suit for Easter every single year. Now what am I supposed to do? I'm going to have to pay for it. I can't believe you lost it."

"We'll find it," Debbie said, glad that her voice came out much calmer than she felt.

"Will you?" Gloria's tone was acerbic. "Like the missing Morrow pearls? Have you found them yet?"

Debbie swallowed hard.

But before she could respond, Rose interjected, "Have you heard anything else about the pearls?"

Debbie sighed. "Not yet. Beatrice is very understanding." *Unlike her nephew.*

"I've got my suspicions about who took them." Agatha shot a glare in Gloria's direction. "Weren't you sneaking around Debbie's house, peering into everything? Maybe *you* saw something unusual."

The suggestion threatened to start another battle. One Debbie didn't have patience for, considering the last meeting held at her house. She raised her hands to plead for order.

Gloria's neck and cheeks flared bright red. "I'm not the person misplacing everything," she snapped, but her fingers tapping against the armrest suggested that the implication might have hit a nerve.

"Debbie's got a lot on her plate," Janet cut in. "Let's cut her some slack. She didn't ask to take care of the suit, Gloria. You could have kept it at your house or your shop until we were actually ready to use it."

"I thought Debbie would wear it," Gloria retorted.

"She has repeatedly refused to do that," Janet pointed out.

"Fine," Gloria said. "But if Debbie needs help, she should say so. I, for one, would like to call for her resignation as chairperson of the Easter committee. It's obviously more than she can handle right now. I'll gladly take over in the meantime, if everyone wants to vote on it." She aimed a smug glance in Debbie's direction.

Debbie scrambled for a response. She was hurt and angry that Gloria would say such a thing in front of the committee—so much so that her brain refused to produce an appropriate reply.

But Rose saved her from having to say anything. "I think Debbie's doing a fine job, considering the fact that none of us wanted to lead in the first place. It's easy to forget that and criticize her when we're not walking in her shoes." Rose turned to Debbie. "I hope you don't mind me asking, but have you discovered anything about the lost train treasure?"

Debbie had never felt so relieved to have a change of subject. However, she had tried to keep her interest in the train robbery as discreet as she could. "How do you know about that?"

"Vicky talked about it when she was asking me if I knew anything about the various historical sites around town. She and Richard are pretty chummy, you know. By the way, where is she? I haven't seen her since our first meeting here two weeks ago."

"Vicky's interest in the heist might be research motivated," Debbie answered slowly. "Vicky and Beatrice want to write a memoir of Morrow House. I'm sure Beatrice has Vicky doing all kinds of digging—the fact-seeking kind. And from what I understand, Vicky and Richard were classmates."

She refused to be further embroiled in gossip. Thankfully, the meeting returned to business, although she couldn't help sneaking a peek in Gloria's direction.

For once, Gloria seemed uncomfortable. She caught Debbie's side glance and frowned.

"I've got to run, ladies. By the way, I happen to know that Greg is building something beautiful for our float." Gloria gathered her purse. "I popped by his house earlier to see the construction with his sons. They've got quite a mess going, but I think it will be perfect for the parade. I'll swing by his place on my way home and let you all know how the progress is going."

Gloria looked pointedly at Debbie and smirked as she slung her bag over her shoulder. She snatched a few of the brochures from the coffee table before leaving. "I'll distribute these around town too. Good night."

"Do you need more help, Debbie?" Agatha asked in the uncomfortable silence that followed Gloria's departure. "Maybe we've left too much on your hands."

"We do need to divide the eggs and candy between us and get them filled," Debbie said. "And then I need to see what I can do about the bunny suit."

Rose shook her head, her expression determined. "No, I'm going to take care of the suit. I'll be wearing it, so I'll make sure it's actually at the parade. You concentrate on the submission forms for the floats. I doubt we'll get many more, but there are always a few stragglers. I'll handle Gloria and her suit, and the flowers too."

"And I'll take care of filling the eggs," Agatha said firmly. "I have granddaughters who would love that job."

Debbie felt the tension seep from her shoulders. "Thank you," she said, feeling tears come to her eyes.

After Rose and Agatha left, Debbie reached for her phone while Janet cleaned up the last of the papers on the coffee table.

She texted Greg. How's the float coming? Do you need anything? She could wield a hammer, but there wasn't much more she could do. Perhaps it was silly to worry that Greg actually welcomed Gloria's intrusions, but she couldn't help it.

Greg texted right back. I'm thinking we should rent a classic car for the commerce entry. I don't think I'll have time to build an actual float after all. I'm sorry.

No problem. I was asking because Gloria said she saw you building something at your house.

Greg's immediate text brought a flash of relief. No way could I construct a float in my garage. I don't have that kind of space. I'm fixing a cabinet. My kids thought they saw her drive by the house slowly. We wondered why.

Debbie typed back, Be warned—she might swing by for a second round.

His responding emoji of a scared face made her giggle. But his next text brought a flutter to her chest. Have you eaten yet? If you haven't, would you like to have dinner at Buona Vita? The boys have plans to meet with their friends for a movie. Buona Vita is much better than my frozen leftovers.

"I love seeing you smile," Janet said as she surveyed Debbie's tidied living room. "Tell me you have good news."

"I guess Greg isn't building a float, and he might be getting irked with Gloria's insinuations. Whatever she's planning, it isn't working."

"Good. We've had our fill of drama."

Debbie sent a quick message to Greg. I'm almost finished with committee work. How about in 30 minutes?

Another text appeared on Debbie's phone, but it wasn't from Greg. It was from Julia Cooper.

Here are the classified ads I wanted you to see. I read them again, and, honestly, they still don't make sense to me. Maybe they will to you. The first one in particular always puzzled me. It says, 'Forgive me. I wish I had more courage.'

"Come and see Julia's photos." Debbie sat on her couch and patted the seat beside her.

Janet joined her, tucking a strand of hair behind her ear.

Debbie zoomed in on the first photo from the *Plain Dealer* and saw the line about courage. Then she swiped to the second.

He said to his friend, "If the British march
By land or sea from the town to-night,
Hang a lantern aloft in the belfry-arch
Of the North-Church-tower, as a signal-light,—
One if by land, and two if by sea;
And I on the opposite shore will be,
Ready to ride and spread the alarm
Through every Middlesex village and farm,
For the country-folk to be up and to arm."

Debbie mulled over the words. "It's from a poem we learned in middle school, remember? It's been ages since I've read it, but this is 'Paul Revere's Ride' by Henry Wadsworth Longfellow."

"That's a poem about the British invading. Why on earth would Myrtle Cooper send it to her son?" Janet asked. "What was she trying to tell him?"

"Your guess is as good as mine," Debbie replied as she reread the words. "Myrtle placed the ad on February 17, 1942. Why couldn't she call her son? Why did she have to communicate through the papers?"

"Good question," Janet said, rubbing the back of her neck. "Do you remember any more details from the articles you read about the heist?"

"The man who was caught claimed that his three cohorts escaped. Gavin Schroeder, another man named Sylvester Alberto, and a female. Everything points to the female being Myrtle. Alberto stopped a car on the tracks, and the guy who was caught feigned choking in the dining car to distract the passengers. He was arrested at the next train stop."

"Did Myrtle send any more messages to her son? Or was it just that one?"

Debbie swiped back to the first photo. "She sent a total of four messages—or, at least, that's how many Walter found. Here's the first one, placed on January twentieth. 'Forgive me. I wish I had more courage.'"

Janet frowned. "Courage to do what? I would think it's pretty courageous to rob a train. But what do you think she did with the loot? Why do people think it might be still in Dennison? Wouldn't she have taken it with her?"

"It's possible, but either way, she returned to Dennison that night, if only to get her things from the boardinghouse. Louise Morrow saw her, remember? Myrtle snuck out of the house without paying her bill, and they never saw her again. Maybe she hid the stolen goods somewhere in the Morrow House. Maybe she wanted her son to find it. Let's look at the third message." She swiped to it. "This one is dated March fourth. 'Could we dig up this long-buried treasure, were it worth the pleasure?'"

Janet whipped out her phone. "Just wait. I'll look it up." A few seconds later, she said, "It's from Oscar Wilde's poem 'Roses and Rue.'"

"This one is pretty obvious, isn't it?" Goose bumps flared across Debbie's skin. "Myrtle is telling her son that she left the treasure somewhere for him, right? It's like she wants him to follow a trail of breadcrumbs."

Janet stood and started to pace. "A warning to watch for the British. A call to dig up treasure. A woman desperate to communicate with her son in code. Perhaps she needed him to get the treasure for her." Janet halted, her eyes gleaming with excitement. "It's got to exist, Debbie. The train robbery loot must be somewhere in Dennison or nearby. She stole it and hid it, and then she had to run. Or maybe she quarreled with the man who helped her—Gavin something, right? Maybe he threatened her."

Debbie exhaled slowly. Maybe Myrtle was the villain. Maybe she had faded away because it was too dangerous to communicate with her son.

Or maybe she'd found her end at the hands of her partner in crime.

"It's quite the crime," Janet continued to mutter to herself. "She must have fooled everyone. The women at the Morrow House. The local pastor. Our very own Harry."

"We don't know that," Debbie reminded her.

She pulled up the last classified ad Myrtle had sent her son. It was dated April 4, 1942. It was a poem that Debbie's mother had hanging on her living room wall. Written by Orson F. Whitney, "The Soul's Captain" was a rebuttal to "Invictus," written by another poet, William Ernest Henley, who declared no one, including God, would ever rule over him.

In contrast, Whitney wrote of the true captain of the soul.

Of what avail thy vaunted strength
Apart from His vast might?
Pray that His light may pierce the gloom

That thou mayest see aright.
Men are as bubbles on the wave,
As leaves upon the tree,
Thou, captain of thy soul! Forsooth,
Who gave that place to thee?
Free will is thine—free agency,
To wield for right or wrong;
But thou must answer unto Him
To whom all souls belong.

This was not the sort of poem a villain would send as a last message. Who, then, was Myrtle Cooper?

CHAPTER TWENTY-ONE

Myrtle ran. Her lungs burned as she gulped icy air. Snowflakes stung her cheeks, and the wind blew straight at her, slowing her down when she most needed speed.

But the wind and the curtain of snow did one other thing. With any luck, it hid her from view.

She'd heard a cry behind her when she'd jumped from the train car with the package. All thoughts of keeping it free of wrinkles evaporated as she fled for her life.

Each step in the powdery drifts felt as if she waded through molasses. She had lost some of her edge, but the years of fencing lessons had strengthened her leg muscles, and she had always made certain to exercise in the penitentiary. She wished she'd done more, but she had hardly anticipated this situation while she was locked up.

In front of her, a row of ice-covered hay bales offered shelter. She ducked behind one to catch her breath. Peeking around the compacted straw, she saw nothing but the gathering white and the faint outline of the train. The stranger who'd dropped his newspaper had seen her running. And he had looked straight into her eyes at the station. Did he recognize her? Why did everything feel like a trap?

Although her legs burned with the effort, she forced herself to move again. Perhaps Gavin would overpower the man in the fedora. Perhaps one of them would die in the struggle. Or perhaps both of them would chase her.

Her husband had drilled into her the rules of what to do if a heist went wrong. "If your accomplice gets caught, keep moving. Especially if you already have the goods."

She certainly had this prize. And whether she followed her husband's rules or not, she couldn't let it fall into the hands Gavin intended it for.

She had one mission left. Run.

She tightened her grip on the envelope and forced herself to break into another jog, her snowshoes making barely any sound on the ground. In front of her, a stand of trees promised shelter. Beyond them, the getaway car awaited with the key in the ignition. She pressed on, ducking between the outstretched branches, and forced herself to be grateful for the brief respite from the wind.

The car, a faint blue color, stood out against the once-red barn. When she reached the driver's door, she dropped the envelope. Her pulse kicked up a notch as she tried to reclaim the package with her clumsy mittens. Finally, she ripped off one mitten and snatched up the envelope, shaking the snow loose. Please, God, let the contents be undamaged.

If only Walter knew what she held in her hand. She took off her snowshoes, yanked the car door open, and carefully, reverently, laid the envelope on the passenger side of the bench, while breathing a sigh of relief when she saw the key in the ignition.

She got in and turned the key. The engine turned over and then, just as quickly, it stalled.

Meanwhile, the snow fell harder. She glanced outside the driver's window, waiting for the dreaded figures to burst through the trees and demand she hand over the goods.

"Don't think about that, Myrtle," she told herself. "Keep moving."

She turned the key one more time, and the engine roared to life.

Jack had never felt so helpless. One minute he saw the woman run into the swirling wind, and the next, she had vanished.

The man beneath him wiggled partially free despite the handcuff clinging to one brawny wrist.

Jack leaned all his weight onto his captive, earning a grunt.

Could he catch her too? Could he somehow handcuff this man to something solid and go after her?

"Tell me where you were headed."

The man growled low in his throat.

"Tell me, Schroeder." Jack enjoyed watching the thief's eyes widen with dismay.

"How do you know my name?" the man rasped.

"You've got a mole. I'll let you figure out who it is."

"It was her, wasn't it?" Gavin bucked again, but Jack was ready for it.

He pressed down on Gavin's chest with his knee. "What's the runner's name? I'll find her eventually, but it might go easier for you if you tell me."

Gavin sneered. "Myrtle Cooper. You might know her as Mimi Jarman. But you better get to her before me, because if I get to her first, she won't be able to tell you anything. She's gonna wish she'd never met me." The flash of distilled hatred in his eyes echoed the sentiment.

Jack recognized the name Mimi Jarman. But Mimi hadn't betrayed Schroeder. It was Renee, the librarian from the Library of Congress, who had kept careful tabs on the crook's operations. Sweet Renee with the charming French accent.

His partner, Larry, burst through the storage door. "The car's moving. It's no longer blocking the tracks. What's happening here?" His gaze darted over the scene and the man beneath Jack.

It all happened so quickly, Jack barely registered it. Gavin slammed his fist into Jack's nose. A throbbing pain brought tears to his eyes, blinding him. The sound of feet scrabbling made him grasp at the air. When his vision finally cleared, he saw Gavin leaping through the open door of the railcar, the snowshoes abandoned behind him.

The distraction had been enough for Gavin to escape. Now Jack had two thieves on the loose. He pivoted to his partner. "Go back and get the man who was choking in the dining car. Hurry!"

Larry's mouth opened in confusion, but he dashed to obey.

As Jack pushed himself to his feet, he prayed they wouldn't be too late.

Night had fallen by the time Myrtle eased into Dennison. She parked the car several blocks from Morrow House, grabbed the envelope, and jogged the rest of the way, thankful for the thick-soled boots on her feet even though they chafed her heels.

The wind picked up, moaning and harsh. She didn't see how she could leave town tonight. But neither could she stay at Morrow House. It would be only a matter of hours before someone found her. Gavin knew where she was staying, and he would check for her there first. Hopefully, he would be under lock and key—if that had been a cop who had burst into the storage car. Maybe Gavin had competition for the package. Maybe the Nazis weren't patiently waiting for the goods. Why pay Gavin when they could steal it too?

Despite her burning lungs, she forced herself to keep moving, as she had done when scaling the prison walls. Weeks ago, aided by the cover of darkness, she had hidden wherever she could find shelter. She could do it again. Anything to protect Walter.

Night wrapped around her like a heavy blanket, but she knew the path to Morrow House from memory, thanks to learning each street and each business. The grand Victorian home loomed ahead of her, the windows black but for a golden sliver of light creeping beneath a pulled curtain.

Esmé rarely locked the door to the kitchen, preferring to keep it open with a lamp on for the odd straggler, although she insisted on a curfew of nine o'clock. The kitchen was unusually quiet. And then it hit her. Esmé had talked about another church function tonight—something about a special Bible study. The house would be empty, and no one would see her enter or leave.

She blew out a relieved breath as she wiped her boots clean before removing them. No sense in leaving a muddy trail on the hardwood floors. Meanwhile, her mind felt as if a tornado ripped through it, rendering her useless. She needed to hide the package. She dared not leave it in the house. How could she endanger the woman who had been so kind to her?

But where else could she stash it? If she was caught with it… Myrtle's mouth dried at the thought of solitary confinement, the pitch-black darkness, and the taunts of the prison guards. She couldn't go back. She couldn't turn herself in, as Walter had suggested. He didn't realize what he was asking of her.

Her footsteps echoed as she walked to the phone in the hall. When she dialed Walter's number, a woman answered. Walter's foster mother.

"Is Walter home?" Myrtle asked.

"Who's calling?" the woman asked.

"I'm a friend," Myrtle said after a pause, her heart pounding in an unsteady rhythm. She didn't have time to argue with this woman who was trying to protect Walter. Nor did she have time to wait for Walter to come to the phone. "Tell him a friend called about the lake house."

She hung up before the woman could reply and then reached to touch the pearls at her throat. The pearls her mother used to wear. What would Mama do in such a situation?

For one thing, she would never leave a bill unpaid.

Myrtle snatched a piece of paper and a pen from the kitchen countertop. An empty tin lay discarded nearby. She would place the pearls inside and leave an apology note for her kind hostess.

But just as she reached for the tin, the outside door to the kitchen swung open. Esmé laughed with delight, her cheeks pink with the cold and her eyes bright as she brushed snow from her coat. "Myrtle, you're back! What happened? Did you miss your train?"

Myrtle schooled her features. "The storm was more than I wanted to risk. I hope you don't mind if I stay a while longer?"

Esmé unwrapped her scarf. The other women filed into the kitchen, their friendly chatter filling the room with a warmth that suddenly felt dangerous to her. It would be all too easy to forget who she was and what she'd done. All too easy to allow herself to sink back into their camaraderie. A fatal mistake.

"No, it's my pleasure. I'm sorry you missed the Bible study. Pastor Darrel almost canceled it." Esmé tucked a strand of hair behind her reddened ear. "Ladies, head to the drawing room, and we'll light a fire in the fireplace. Someone can read while I make tea for everyone."

Myrtle headed upstairs to her room, clutching the tin. She sat down at her desk and unfolded the blank piece of paper she'd found. As she tried to figure out what to write, she glanced up at the window where the garden lay covered in darkness, and near it, the ice-house. And in the distance, a steeple . . .

Her breath caught as an idea took form. A ridiculous idea, but since she had so few choices . . .

Unclasping the pearls from around her neck, she wrapped her handkerchief around them and slid them into the tin. Then she scribbled a line on the paper, folded it, and placed it on top of the handkerchief. It felt strange to part with the pearls like this. But it also felt right. She would pay Esmé with what she had. Her meager stash of money was far more important to her survival than the pearls. She had just enough to get to some small town. Somewhere in New Mexico, perhaps? Texas? A border town close to Mexico might be the best.

She'd avoid the big cities. Somehow. She could hitchhike at least part of the way.

One step at a time.

She glanced at the window again, shivering at her gaunt and distorted reflection in the rippled glass. Could she somehow mail the stolen envelope to the rightful owners? The post office opened early in the morning. No, she couldn't afford to wait that long. Indecision filled her. She could take it with her. Or she could hide it.

Sell it, hissed a selfish voice in her mind. Sell it and make a fortune and take Walter to Mexico.

But minutes ticked past, every second heavier than the last, as she struggled to breathe in the small bedroom. Finally, her mind cleared. She would ask Esmé for a bread box, and the rest… well, it would sort itself out.

And she would get out of Dennison before dawn.

CHAPTER TWENTY-TWO

*T*he café experienced an uptick in orders on Friday. Debbie filled yet another white pastry box with sugar cookies shaped like rabbits or birds with royal icing. Janet's pastel cookies sold as quickly as she baked them.

She rang up the most recent sale then slid the box across the counter to the customer.

Paulette refilled a coffeepot. She cleared her throat as the customer left. "Debbie, I've been meaning to chat with you about something."

Debbie paused at the uncertainty in the older woman's voice. "Sure. What about?"

Paulette frowned. "I don't know how to say this, but I've been hearing some gossip around town, and it's very upsetting."

"Oh?" Debbie bit her lip. She had fielded plenty of questions about the pearls, the bunny suit, and the parade. She braced herself for the next round of that.

"Gloria's a talker. Not that I place much faith in what others say, but she's been…" Paulette blew out a breath then said in a rush, "Well, Harry overheard her in the grocery story saying she's going to ask Greg out. Do you know anything about that? I left a message for Greg this morning, but he's so busy, and he hasn't called back."

"I have no idea what plans Gloria has," Debbie said slowly. "I think she's a bit—"

"Pushy? Yes, that's my concern as well." Paulette appraised her for a moment and then said, "Don't let her get away with it, Debbie."

Paulette left Debbie stammering at the counter with heat suffusing her cheeks. She grabbed her phone and impulsively dialed Greg's number. No answer. Chiding herself, she ignored the voice mail prompt, hung up, and stuffed the phone back into her pocket. After all, what could she do? It wasn't as if she was his girlfriend.

But her heart was telling her something else. The night before, when they'd gone to dinner at Buona Vita, she thought for sure a couple of times that he'd wanted to say something to her and then changed his mind. Could he be thinking about taking their relationship beyond the friend zone?

At closing time, she decided to take a box of cookies to Beatrice. She wanted to do something nice, but she also wanted to discuss Myrtle's coded messages with her former teacher. Perhaps Beatrice would have some insight she hadn't yet thought of. Janet and Paulette offered to close the café so she could leave sooner.

The break felt wonderful as she drove toward Morrow House. The cookies smelled divine, filling the car with the scent of sugar and vanilla. As she pulled up to the Victorian house, another car eased out of the driveway. A red luxury sedan, with a familiar driver wearing an ivory coat.

Cecilia Belanger, the appraiser. Her frantic gaze collided with Debbie's for a split second before the car zoomed away. Why had Cecilia come to Morrow House, and why was she in such a hurry to leave?

Puzzled, Debbie climbed out of her car with the box of cookies in hand. She went to the door and rapped it with the brass knocker.

The door opened, and Beatrice looked at Debbie's box of cookies with open delight. "Debbie, what a pleasant surprise."

Debbie gestured toward the street. "I've brought treats and news. Was that Cecilia I saw leaving the house?"

"Come in." Beatrice stood back. "You're welcome here, unlike that vulture."

"What happened?" Debbie asked as she followed Beatrice into the hall. She rarely heard the sweet-tempered woman speak with such vitriol.

"My nephew told her he might have things of interest to her besides the pearls. Of course he has nothing yet. I don't know what he promised her, but he told her he's looking for the lost train treasure, and now she wants dibs on whatever he finds. I'm tired of telling her no. She's so—"

"Pushy," Debbie supplied with a wink. Cecilia and Gloria had that in common. "I've been encountering that trait in someone else recently."

Beatrice chuckled as she slipped her arm through Debbie's. "Bring those cookies, and let's console each other over tea. You can tell me what you've found so far."

Debbie glanced around for Richard, hoping he wouldn't inject himself into the visit, but the house felt abnormally quiet. "Are you alone today? Where are Richard and Vicky?"

Beatrice shrugged. "Richard is filling out paperwork for a job. Vicky offered to pick up a prescription and some milk for me. She should be back any minute."

Debbie sat down at the kitchen table. The Morrow kitchen hadn't changed over the years. Glass knobs sparkled on the cupboard doors, and the window, framed with lacy curtains, let in plenty of sunlight.

Beatrice bustled around the room, getting tea together. "What can I do for you today, Debbie?"

"I wanted to share some coded messages with you. I received them from Myrtle's granddaughter. I understand Myrtle disappeared after that snowstorm in January 1942, which incidentally, was also after the train robbery. According to her granddaughter, she sent her son, Walter, mysterious messages and poems in the classified section of the *Plain Dealer*, but he never understood what she was trying to say. I was hoping you'd take a look and tell me what you think." Debbie slid her phone to Beatrice with the first classified ad displayed on the screen.

Beatrice fished for the chain around her neck and put on her gold reading glasses. Her brow wrinkled as she scrolled through the messages. "If this isn't the strangest thing I've seen all day."

"I think Myrtle did something with the treasure, and those messages are code for where she hid it."

Beatrice handed back the phone. "Did you say you saw the article that was in the paper back then about the train robbery?"

"I have it right here," said Debbie. She'd printed out the entire twelve-page edition of the January 13, 1942, paper and stuffed it into her purse on her way out of the library. She'd had no time in the last three days to look at it closer.

Beatrice took the papers and paged through them until she came to the article about the train robbery. She handed the rest of the pages back to Debbie.

While Beatrice read the article, Debbie shuffled the remaining pages back in order. As she did so, the front-page headline caught her eye. BLACK CAT STILL ON THE LOOSE. A grainy black-and-white photograph accompanied the article, and Debbie looked closely at it. The woman looked familiar. The hair was lighter, and the face was more youthful, but…

She grabbed her phone again and scrolled through her gallery to the picture of the women in front of the fireplace at the Morrow House. The woman's hair was darker, and she looked older, but it was the same woman. Myrtle Cooper was Mimi Jarman, aka the Black Cat.

Beatrice looked up from her reading. "Do you remember I told you about my mother seeing someone leave the house the night of the robbery?" When Debbie nodded, Beatrice said, "I remembered last night that she said the person went to the icehouse before they left. Do you think…?"

Debbie rose from the table and peered out the window over the sink. Was the icehouse the missing piece of the puzzle?

"What do you say we go check it out?" she asked, attempting to keep her voice level and failing.

Beatrice's jaw dropped. "Do you really think the lost treasure is in there?"

"Why not? And what do we have to lose if it isn't?"

Beatrice stood from the kitchen table, leaving a half-eaten cookie on her plate. "It might be dangerous to go in there. The icehouse hasn't been used in decades. I really ought to tear it down and use the space for a garden, as Richard has suggested. But I don't have the heart to destroy any of the property's history yet. And my budget is limited."

"If it is a hazard, you should deal with it as soon as possible," Debbie said gently.

Something hanging from the eaves of the icehouse caught her attention.

"Is that an old lantern? Hanging outside the entrance to the icehouse?"

Beatrice joined Debbie at the window, and stood on her tiptoes. The former teacher pushed up her glasses to see better. "Yes, I think you're right."

The line in Walter Revere's poem reverberated through Debbie. *Hang a lantern aloft...*

Were they finally on the right track?

The icehouse perhaps presented one of the most dangerous situations Debbie had ever encountered. The sod-covered roof, bursting with fresh grass, appeared on the verge of collapse, with the middle portion sagging so low, it would touch her head. If she went in there, she might never come out again. Normally she wasn't one to get squeamish with tight spaces, but the situation was hardly normal. And, normally, she wouldn't even consider entering a building that was likely to collapse at the slightest provocation. Not to mention the oozing mud inside and the critters that might be slithering through it.

She inched toward the opening, a black hole barely big enough for her to wiggle through. Shining the light of her phone into the damp and earthy interior, she studied the ground for any abnormalities.

Had the treasure been buried in there? There was no way to know for sure without getting up close and personal.

"Richard wanted to crawl in there, but I think he had trouble." Beatrice folded her arms across her chest, while the cool spring wind tousled her short hair.

Debbie studied the perimeter of the icehouse. Large footprints circled the structure. A crumbling line of disturbed earth near the opening revealed that Richard had tried to enter and given up, likely finding the opening too small to accommodate him.

Dare she crawl inside? She'd ruin her clothes. Then again, it might be worth it if she did happen to find the treasure.

With a muttered prayer, Debbie eased into the structure in spite of Beatrice's yelp, holding her cell phone aloft to shine its flashlight on the muddy walls.

"We haven't had an ice delivery since the sixties. No one's done maintenance on the place since then," Beatrice fussed. "Oh, honey, I don't have a good feeling about you being in there."

Debbie chuckled. Her shoes were already coated with mud. "Me neither. Keep talking, Beatrice. It gives me something else to focus on."

Beatrice took a deep breath, and then a familiar tone came into her voice—her teaching tone. "This icehouse is truly historic, as is the glass conservatory. Ezekiel, who built the house and the accompanying buildings, wanted the nicest home in all of Ohio for his young bride. With no refrigerator back then, he built this. You know, I could restore it and maybe treat it as a tourist attraction."

"I imagine that would be even more expensive than taking it down," Debbie murmured to herself. The walls appeared smooth, with no indentations that she could see. However, a button lay on the ground, ivory colored and almost pearlescent. She picked it up and made her way back outside, her jeans covered in mud.

"I found something." She held it out on her palm.

Beatrice picked up the button and studied it. "It's new, I think. But it's not Richard's button. Too feminine. Who else has been here?"

Debbie rubbed her palms on her jeans, thinking of Cecilia and her cream-colored wardrobe. "I didn't see anything else in there, and there's no signs of something being buried or hidden. Do you think the button might belong to Cecilia?"

Beatrice's mouth gaped. "I thought I'd gotten her to leave, but what if she's been sneaking around out here behind my back?"

"I only saw her drive off," Debbie said. "She could have been muddy, for all I know. She certainly didn't want to say hello to me. She sped out of your driveway as if someone was chasing her."

Beatrice sighed. "If she found something, we'll probably never know it. Let's go back in the house and get you cleaned up."

"Good idea. I'll try not to get mud all over your kitchen." Debbie glanced at the lantern and paused. It was rusted, the glass cracked with age. She picked it up and examined the bottom. She could make out a brand name—Coleman. Kim kept a collection in the museum, most of them from World War II, and she thought this one was similar to those.

But that didn't prove anything. A lantern was a perfectly logical thing to have handy when you wanted to go into an icehouse.

Then a thought struck her. It was January when the train was robbed and Myrtle left the house. And it was during a snowstorm. The ground would have been frozen solid. Surely she wouldn't have had the time or the equipment to dig a hole.

Besides, Myrtle had stayed only long enough to scribble a note and leave it with her pearls in the tin. Those were not the actions of a woman who had the time to find the best place to hide her hoard. But there was no denying Myrtle had hidden something somewhere. Something so serious that she would risk blowing her cover attempting to tell her son about it.

When Debbie entered the house, she found a small bathroom off the kitchen and washed her hands in the sink. Beatrice remained outside, scouring the grounds for more clues.

Cecilia had been at the house earlier, wearing an ivory jacket. Would she have resorted to crawling on her hands and knees in the mud to get to the treasure?

What if Richard had found something and given it to Cecilia without Beatrice's knowledge? Morrow House was huge. Beatrice could have been busy in another room while Richard—or Cecilia operating on her own—entered the property and stole something of interest.

Debbie dried her hands and went back into the kitchen as a sound echoed down the hall. She glanced out the window and saw that Beatrice was still outside. Holding her breath, she tiptoed the length of the carpet. The former parlor sat across from the dining room, which had been partially converted into an office. A woman's blond ponytail bounced as she opened the rolltop desk. She wore a baggy denim shirt over navy yoga pants.

Vicky.

The young ghostwriter rummaged through the desk, pulling out folded documents and other things. She slipped out her phone and snapped pictures.

"Hey, Vicky," Debbie called from the doorway.

Vicky dropped her phone on the desk with a clatter. She whirled around, her face pale. "Debbie, I didn't expect to see you today. How goes the search for the pearls?"

"It's been interesting," Debbie answered slowly. What exactly was Vicky searching for? Did she have Beatrice's permission to go rummaging through personal papers?

"If you need help, let me know," Vicky said, clearly trying to sound light and breezy. "Did I tell you we may have found a publisher willing to take on Bea's book?"

"That's wonderful news." Debbie gestured toward the desk. "Are you retrieving something for her?"

Vicky glanced at the papers on the desk and blushed. "The pharmacy said they didn't have a record of her prescription. I need to find the copy the doctor gave her and take it to them."

"I'm sure Beatrice could call the doctor's office and have them resend the prescription to the pharmacy."

Vicky shook her head. "Beatrice works the old-school way. She gets all her prescriptions in writing. It has to be somewhere on her desk. I don't want to bother her." Then she held up a slip of pink paper that was in plain sight on the desk. "Here it is. Problem solved." She rushed out of the dining room, throwing over her shoulder, "Will you let Bea know I'll be late?"

The door slammed, and Debbie was alone in the hall, mulling over the strange conversation. Beatrice had admitted that she'd sent

Vicky for the medication. But it still felt strange, especially considering the visit from Cecilia.

Had Vicky told the truth? Whose button was in the icehouse? Vicky's denim shirt had blue buttons. Not ivory.

But there was no telling how long the button had been there.

Debbie ran a hand through her hair. It seemed the more clues she found, the muddier everything got.

CHAPTER TWENTY-THREE

Dennison, Ohio
January 12, 1942

Darrel exited his church office while the wind howled outside. He paused by the light switch in the sanctuary, eyeing the storm raging outside the church. Clara had stayed home this evening, nursing a cold. Hattie had left on the train for warmer weather farther south a few days before, and had called to let them know she'd arrived safely. Darrel was glad she'd left ahead of the snowstorm.

Despite the forecast, Darrel had been loath to cancel his Bible study. If someone needed guidance and comfort, he would make sure they received it. He'd reminded his congregation of the weather and asked them to take it into account when deciding whether to attend. To his surprise, Esmé Morrow came with her boarders, along with a few others. No Myrtle Cooper, much to his disappointment.

Esmé told him that Myrtle had left on a train right before the storm hit. He mulled over the strange man he'd seen with her. Already, Darrel had heard gossip around town about the flashy visitor and how unpleasant he was.

Had the man forced Myrtle to leave with him?

The very idea brought a sour taste to his mouth. He flipped the light switch, plunging the church into darkness while the wind howled against the stained glass windows. All he had left to do was to lock the church doors and return to his wife, who was probably already asleep in bed. Why did he feel moved to linger? To pray?

The more the storm raged outside, the more he felt as if his soul wrestled with something dark, something far beyond the church. He obeyed the call to pray and knelt before the altar until the feeling lessened. Finally, utterly exhausted and with aching knees, he rose and made his way out of the sanctuary. He fumbled for his coat hanging on a hook at the entrance of the church.

Footsteps pattered softly behind him. He froze for a second then realized it might be better for whoever it was to believe he hadn't heard.

Holding his breath, he grabbed his hat from the coatrack and placed it on his head. Another footstep came from behind him, where the staircase led up to the balcony.

After a moment he moved to the bottom of the steps and cleared his throat. "I know you are there. No need to be so quiet. You have nothing to fear here. If you need a place to stay, I'll help you find something better than a pew."

A sharp intake of breath.

Darrel forced himself to hold still. His stomach clenched when he saw Myrtle descend the stairs. She wore pants and her usual long, shapeless coat.

"Myrtle? Weren't you supposed to be on the train?"

It was hard to make out her expression in the shadows. A light flashed across the stained glass windows, long and brilliant, like that of a car's headlights.

"Get away from the door," she hissed at him, motioning for him to follow her behind the stairs.

"What's going on, Myrtle?"

A rumble of a car engine filtered faintly through the door. Myrtle grabbed his arm and tugged him deeper into the shadows. The church door rattled then opened. Snow blew in, and the shape of a man filled the doorway, framed by the glow of the headlights.

"She'd be an idiot to hide in here," a gruff voice protested, but the man at the door didn't budge.

"You don't know her like I do."

"It's snowing like crazy. We'll be stuck here and caught if you don't hurry," the other man snarled. "She's gone. Long gone. Let it go."

The man in the doorway turned his face, and Darrel gasped when he recognized the man he'd seen with Myrtle. Her fingers dug into his arm in a clear warning.

The man stepped inside the church, ignoring his companion. Darrel's heart nearly exploded in his chest. Fortunately, the stranger gave but a cursory glance into the sanctuary before he apparently thought better of it.

"Let's move," he barked to the other man. The door slammed shut behind them.

Darrel clutched at the banister. "I'm going to lock the door, and then I think you and I need to talk."

His fingers were clumsy, and he dropped his key before he managed to secure the door. Then he joined Myrtle, who, to her credit, hadn't moved. Would he be able to get the truth from her?

"I'm running away." Myrtle's soft answer surprised him. "I was hiding in the tower when I heard you downstairs. I thought perhaps I could sleep on a pew and leave in the morning before anyone found me."

"That man is after you, isn't he? Your husband?"

She didn't answer, instead clasping her hands together.

Darrel didn't press her. "I can't let you stay in the church. It's not warm enough in this weather. Not to mention that I'd never hear the end of it from my wife. She has a cold right now, but there's nothing she wouldn't do for someone in crisis. You can stay with us until you figure out what to do."

"He's a very bad man who has committed more than a few murders. You can't hide me for long. News travels too fast here. He'll hear about it and come back with his friends. I won't put you in his path. I need to leave here by dawn if the roads are clear enough."

Darrel frowned, but he could tell from her expression that there would be no changing her mind. "My wife and I will drive you out of town. Maybe we can get you a bus ticket. Tell me how far to drive, and I'll do it."

She gave him a small smile. "Pastor, I'm not lying to you. Those men are very dangerous. They must never know that you were involved tonight."

"I can keep a secret." He tried to infuse light humor into his tone and failed. "It comes with the territory. I won't reveal what happened tonight to anyone. Not ever."

Early the next morning, Darrel packed the car with essentials. The roads were clear enough for travel, and the drifts were not as bad as he'd feared the previous night. The morning dawn colored the sky in faint tones of pink, and the snow sparkled. It was lovely—or would have been if he wasn't so nervous.

His wife had given Myrtle a dress to wear and other clothing in a suitcase. They'd also ensured that she had food and money. Then they drove her out of Dennison.

In the nearby village of Gnadenhutten, they found a farmer who promised to give Myrtle another ride.

"This will save the money for the bus," she told Darrel as he hefted her suitcase into the back of the rusty pickup truck.

"Where will you go?" he asked, unable to hide his worry for her.

"Wherever the wind blows, Pastor." Her lips quirked with a small smile. Before she entered the truck, she paused. "You really believe people can change?"

"Yes," he answered without hesitation. "But not by might nor by our own strength. It's God who brings the change. You only need to seek Him. Wherever you go, Myrtle, if you go with God, you will never be lost. And you cannot run from His love."

Her smile vanished, but the relief that softened her features was enough to bring him a small measure of peace. He waited inside his warm car until the truck disappeared from sight.

His wife reached out to clasp his hand. "You're a good man, Darrel Armstrong."

He sighed as he squeezed her fingers in return. She had worked at his side for forty years, as much a partner in his ministry as she was in the rest of his life. Some days, he felt like a failure, wondering if the work he did would ever amount to anything fruitful in the small town of Dennison, Ohio. "I don't know, dear. I didn't solve things for Myrtle."

"You did what you could for her, and more than most others would have done," she assured him. "Who knows how one act of kindness will affect someone's life, like ripples in a pond?"

"I thought you wanted me to retire," he teased her as he turned the key in the ignition.

"I do. But I'm proud of you all the same. You're the kind of man who gives until his very last breath. I knew it when I married you, and if I'm honest, it's one of the reasons I did. The world needs more people like you—kind and thoughtful, serving in small and quiet ways, even if no one else sees or applauds."

*He smiled as he eased the car into the nearest lane,
the roads a blinding white beneath the brilliant sun.
And as he returned home, he whispered a prayer that
Myrtle Cooper found a better path to tread.*

*Columbus, Ohio
January 13, 1942*

*Jack called his superior late at night. After the usual
greetings, he cleared his throat and glanced around the
hotel hall for anyone listening. "It's lost. We have one
man in custody. Unfortunately, three birds are heading
south as we speak."*

*A snarl crackled across the line. "Fix it, Jack. Fix
it or face the consequences."*

*He bit his tongue, barely keeping in his snide reply.
Hadn't he asked for more men? Now he was short-
handed and forced to track three criminals who might,
or might not, converge on the same path. "Larry is on
his way to the next train stop, and we caught one bird.
We'll see if we can get it to sing. I've got a few men fan-
ning out to nearby towns."*

"And you? What will you do?"

He thought of the woman sprinting across the snow, the one with the envelope tucked beneath her arm. "I've got a hare to catch." After hanging up, he lowered the brim of his fedora and marched out into the blistering cold.

CHAPTER TWENTY-FOUR

*A*t home on Monday evening, Debbie curled up on her couch and reread the classified ads, particularly "The Midnight Ride of Paul Revere." Then she swiped to the first message, which contained no poetry, but rather a plea.

Forgive me. I wish I had more courage.

Myrtle's small circle of friends in Dennison had included Esmé Morrow. What about Pastor Darrel? Might there be a deeper connection between the two of them, considering his journal entries? Harry's visit to the café had also revealed some intriguing clues, namely that Pastor Darrel refused to discuss Myrtle.

Clearly, the pastor felt the need to protect the woman. Why?

He wouldn't cover up a robbery, would he?

Debbie was about to make a pot of decaf coffee when her phone rang. She answered it as she scooted off the couch.

"Hi, Debbie," Greg said. "How are you holding up?"

She smiled, glad to hear his voice. "It's been an eventful few days since we last talked. Someone stole the bunny suit from my car. I haven't found the pearls yet. And I crawled through the icehouse at Beatrice's."

"You did not!" He sounded horrified. "That thing needs to be condemned."

She cleared her throat. "No arguments here. Beatrice remembers her mother telling her about someone heading toward the icehouse after dark the night of the robbery. We believe she took something from the train based on the news articles."

Briefly, she filled him in about the news articles, the picture of the Black Cat, and the messages in the classifieds as well as the button in the icehouse.

He was silent for a long moment. "I don't know what to say. It does sound like Richard has a reason to hunt for the lost loot. Just please, let me know the next time you want to investigate an older building. I'd feel better if I was there to make sure it's safe before you go in. That's part of my job as head of a construction crew, to keep my employees safe on the worksite."

"Okay," Debbie said, "but I really don't think I was in any great danger in the icehouse."

She heard Greg take a deep breath. "You sound like my foreman," he said. "He was determined to get into that old church to get some measurements before we assessed it for safety, and I had to practically threaten to hog-tie him to keep him from it."

The church... The one that Darrel Armstrong pastored in the forties... Suddenly the Paul Revere poem made sense. Debbie couldn't keep the excitement out of her voice when she said, "One of the messages that Myrtle sent her son was the poem about Paul Revere's ride. 'One if by land, two if by sea.'"

"Yeah," Greg said in a puzzled tone. "You just told me about that. We had to memorize part of it in junior high a hundred years ago."

Realization bloomed in her mind so strongly that she wanted to grab her coat and run all the way to Beatrice so she could share the good news. "You're right," she said. "We all had to memorize or at least study it as kids. And I bet that included Beatrice's son, Walter. Greg, you are the very best!"

"I don't know what I did to make you so happy, but it if worked, I'm delighted." He chuckled. "And I should get going. I promised the boys we'd go out for burgers tonight."

She grinned at his response. "And I've got to call Janet. I'll call you back later and explain everything."

"Great." There was a pause, and then he said, "Debbie, wait. You said the bunny suit is missing? I saw Gloria with it in her car. That bright blue thing with white satin ears, right?"

"*What?*" Debbie squawked.

"Gloria has the suit," he repeated. "I saw it in her trunk today when she was loading groceries. She looked a little embarrassed when she saw me and closed the trunk quickly, but I know I saw it. Why do you think she told you it was lost?"

Debbie gritted her teeth. She had an idea why, but she wouldn't mention it to Greg. Not until she had proof.

Tuesday morning dawned brightly for Debbie despite her lack of sleep. The previous night, she had nearly driven to the old church despite the evening hour and it being closed to the public, but sense had prevailed, and she had decided to wait until she had daylight—and could possibly talk the contractor into allowing her access to the building.

As soon as she woke up, she snatched her phone and called Greg to ask him if she could explore the church he was renovating. He didn't pick up, so she sent a text. She also texted Janet and asked her to call. Then she sent a text to Beatrice to give her an update on the new lead.

Finally, despite the nervous tension in her chest, she called Gloria. The call went straight to voice mail. She left a message, hoping her voice sounded steadier than she felt. "Gloria, Greg said he saw you with the bunny suit. What's going on? Why didn't you tell me and the other members of the committee you had it?"

As she dressed for the day, her phone rang. *Gloria.*

Debbie answered and was surprised when a tearful Gloria stuttered out an apology. "Debbie, I'm so sorry. I took the bunny suit to have it dry-cleaned. You know how busy life can get. I've got a huge order of flowers to manage, and I guess I totally forgot that I had it."

"You took it from my car?"

"Uh, yes, I did."

Gloria's smug accusations filtered through Debbie's memory. "Did you also take Beatrice's pearls the night you wandered through my house?"

A low groan sounded across the line. "I didn't. I would never take something that didn't belong to me. I figured you had so much going on, I'd take the suit back."

"You accused me of losing it in front of the entire committee," Debbie reminded her.

"I—yes. I was frustrated that you were given the role of chairperson. And I was angry that..." Gloria let her voice fade, leaving plenty unsaid.

Debbie steeled herself, recognizing the jealousy in the florist's tone.

"I understand why you might not believe me," Gloria said. "Again, I'm so sorry about the suit. But I didn't take the pearls. You probably should talk to the woman who came into your house the night of our meeting. Not to mention Beatrice's writer. What's her name?"

"Vicky," Debbie answered. "What about her?"

"I saw her go upstairs before I headed to your kitchen with Greg to look at the woodwork."

They said goodbye and Debbie ended the call, more disturbed than ever. She highly doubted Gloria had told the truth. At least she had been exposed for her games around the committee. But who had stolen the pearls? Could it really be Cecilia? Or Vicky? Or was Gloria merely offering misdirection after stealing the bunny suit?

After another busy Tuesday at work, Debbie and Janet headed to the old church. The café had been filled with a constant stream of customers, but despite Debbie's aching feet, she felt a thrill of excitement simply thinking about the church. She had sent another message to Beatrice around lunchtime and was getting worried that her friend hadn't answered. Greg had finally answered her text, agreeing to take her through the old church when he got off that afternoon.

As she drove, Debbie filled Janet in on Myrtle's alias and how she'd found the Black Cat's picture in the newspaper. Janet retrieved the photocopies from Debbie's purse and confirmed the likeness herself.

"Can you imagine if the loot is in the belfry?" Debbie asked, easing the car into a parking spot in front of the brick church. Greg's truck wasn't there, which meant he must still be at another worksite.

"I'm intrigued by the idea of a poem leading to the hiding spot," Janet said. "But why would Myrtle hide it here?"

Debbie shrugged as she opened her car door and got out. "Maybe she felt this was the safest place. She clearly intended for her son to find it. Unfortunately, he wasn't able to decode her clues."

"I wonder if someone stopped Myrtle from coming back for it. Or could she have returned for it herself and lived the rest of her years as a rich woman? Maybe that's why her messages suddenly stopped. She decided to disappear with all of it for herself."

Debbie fairly itched to go inside. "Anything is possible, I suppose. Do you think Greg would be angry if we went in without him?"

"I'm not sure about angry, but given the state of the building, we should wait for him." Janet pointed to a sign that warned the public to keep out. "After all, there are probably safety reasons for that."

"I guess you're right, but maybe we should see if it's locked." Debbie easily pushed open the worn red door to the church, though the rusted hinges creaked loudly. "I'm sure it's fine. Greg will be here any minute." She stepped through the door, ignoring Janet's resigned sigh.

"We have so many questions, don't we?" Debbie mused. "I can't help but wonder about her story. The Black Cat was one of the most famous female criminals of the forties. Do you think she reformed in the end?"

"She never returned to jail, did she?" Janet followed closely.

"Not that I've found."

The interior of the church smelled of sawdust and mold. The ceiling bubbled with water damage, the once-white tiles had turned a rusty brown, and the red carpet was littered with debris from the crumbling walls.

"Poor Greg," Debbie murmured as she glanced around the entrance room. "The stained glass is beautiful, but as for the rest of it—well, he's got his work cut out for him."

"I'm glad the building is getting a new life again as a youth center," Janet said.

The old pews were pushed against the west wall of the sanctuary. The front of the church no longer housed the pulpit, but a few tattered banners hung from the wall. NEW LIFE IN CHRIST, one read.

"New beginnings," Janet said, pointing to it.

"It's a great theme," Debbie said.

Janet pointed to the stairs. "Let's check the belfry, since the poem mentions one," she suggested. She led the way to the staircase and peered up to the balcony. "It must be that way, but I don't know about going all the way to the top. It looks pretty rickety."

Debbie started up the stairs. A violent sneeze racked her, thanks to the dust motes floating in the air. "Stay put. I'll take a quick peek and come right back down."

"No way are you leaving me at the bottom." Janet followed, the old steps creaking under her weight.

Debbie advanced until she came to a small door at the far end of the balcony. She pushed it open and saw a narrow flight of stairs curling to the top of the belfry tower. A groan escaped her. Greg wasn't kidding when he said the building was decrepit. Light peeked through several slats in the roof. Gritting her teeth, she gingerly climbed the stairs, carefully placing her feet on one step at a time while clinging to the iron railing.

At the top, a lantern waited, hanging from a hook on the white-washed wall.

Janet gasped behind her, though Debbie couldn't tell if it was from shock about the lantern's presence or trying to catch her breath. Perhaps it was a combination. "Just like the poem."

Debbie took the lantern down to study it better. It was a Coleman lamp from the World War II era, much like the lamp at the icehouse. Maybe Myrtle had brought it to the church.

Debbie set the lamp back on the hook. Taking a deep breath to calm the fluttering in her stomach, she entered the belfry, where a large bell hung from the rafters.

"Myrtle must have intended for her son to search the Dennison churches and find the lantern," she said as she touched the enormous rim of the bell. "It's a shame she couldn't risk giving him enough information for him to figure it out."

The floorboards protested beneath her weight and Janet's.

"We should leave," Janet said. "The floor is rotten."

Debbie knew her friend was right, but some wooden crates peeked out from under a filthy tarp on the far side of the small room. She inched carefully across the boards as if easing over fragile ice.

Carefully, she knelt and lifted the edge of the tarp, disturbing a thick layer of dust that made her sneeze again. The crates were covered, the tops nailed in place. But one crate had a loose lid. Debbie pushed the lid aside as Janet peered over her shoulder.

A musty smell wafted upward. Debbie reached into the crate, her fingers brushing against metal. Butterflies took flight in her stomach.

She pulled out a long narrow box, holding it up to the faint light filtering through the gaps in the roof and walls.

"It's a bread box," she murmured. Without the use of plastic bags, bread boxes had once been invaluable for storing loaves and protecting against mold.

She carefully flipped it over, her pulse racing at the name etched on the side of the box.

Morrow House.

"Don't leave me in suspense, Debbie. Open it!" Janet said.

Debbie unhooked the latch and raised the lid. Inside lay a large envelope, curled slightly to fit inside the box. She carefully tugged it free. Of all the items she had been expecting, this wasn't one of them. Had she made a mistake assuming Myrtle had hidden treasure in the belfry?

But all thoughts scattered when she took out the first sheet of paper, warped with time, the fading scrawl long and elegant with flourishes no one used anymore.

"No way." Her voice sounded unnaturally loud in her own ears. "This can't be possible."

Janet placed a hand on Debbie's shoulder for balance as she leaned closer.

One of Abraham Lincoln's letters to his wife during the Civil War lay in her hand. Stunned, she could only stare at the priceless document.

"How in the world did Myrtle Cooper end up with that?" Janet whispered.

Debbie pointed to a stamp on the envelope. "The Library of Congress. Somehow, the Black Cat was involved in the heist."

"On a train headed from Dennison, no less," Janet breathed. "There are more pages in there."

Debbie shuffled the papers, her alarm mounting as she skimmed each one. A diary entry from Thomas Jefferson, torn from the pages of a journal. But the last group of papers, folded and compressed to fit the envelope, were the most unbelievable.

Janet uttered a small cry beside Debbie. "This is George Washington's first inaugural speech. What are we going to do?" The question hung in the air as Debbie struggled to think.

Something clanked below, like metal falling. Debbie glanced around the belfry. Greg had warned her about his project. Had someone entered the building? "We have to move. This tower might not hold our weight much longer. Can you send a message to Ian or call 911?"

Janet pulled out her phone. "The signal isn't very good, but I'll try."

Old as it was, the envelope was fragile to the touch. Rather than risk the precious papers to it once more, Debbie tucked the speech into her denim jacket as carefully as she could, since it was likely she would need both hands to descend the rickety staircase. But before she could insert the journal entries and Lincoln's letter into the safety of her jacket, footsteps thundered up the stairs. Whoever was coming was heedless of the danger of rotten boards.

Debbie cried out when Richard's face appeared at the top of the steps.

He held out his hand. "Better get out of the tower. It could collapse any second."

She hesitated, the brittle papers in her hand. "How did you know we were here?"

He exhaled, glancing at the decrepit floor before meeting her gaze again. "I saw the message on Aunt Bea's phone. Whatever you found belongs to her." He spotted the bread box, and his eyes widened. "That says 'Morrow House,' which means it and its contents are definitely my family's property."

Debbie mentally chided herself for leaving Beatrice the detailed message about Myrtle and the church. Could she trust Richard?

With one gigantic step, one that belied his previous warning, he stepped farther into the tower, his hand still outstretched. "I heard Janet say what those papers are. I've been hunting for the train loot day and night. To think it's been here all these years!"

A floorboard gave way, snapping in half beneath his foot. Richard leaped backward, his face pale as part of the belfry floor collapsed. Debbie stared at the gaping hole as sounds of the board clattering down the stairs echoed loudly.

She was about to answer him when more boards plummeted to the ground below. The resulting *thunk, thunk, thunk* sounded like a death knell.

Janet yelped as she stumbled backward.

"Fan out so we can distribute our weight," Debbie ordered as she pressed her back against the nearest wall. Janet did the same, moving left of Debbie. The bell provided a partial barrier between them and Richard.

From the safety of the stairs, he extended his hand a second time. "Give me the papers, Debbie. Give them to me, and I'll help you get to safety. If you don't, I'll make sure this floor collapses completely." He sneered. "And I'll get them anyway."

"You have to give them to him," Janet said, clinging to the wall. "We can't stay here. The entire floor is about to go."

"Can you call Ian one more time?" Debbie asked her friend.

"I'm not going to wait for Ian," Richard snapped. "I'm here. Hand over the papers, and I promise, I'll help you."

"Why should we trust you?" Debbie asked.

"What's your alternative?" Richard scowled at her. "Now, Debbie."

Biting her lip, Debbie glanced again at Janet, who nodded her approval. With careful steps, she slid her back along the wall, avoiding the gaping center where the boards dipped toward the hole.

"Good job," Richard coaxed, his face creasing into a smile. "You're doing great."

She held out the documents she hadn't been able to hide, the Jefferson diary entry and the Lincoln letters.

Richard grabbed them, his large hand brushing against her fingertips. He glanced at the top page and then stepped backward. She could easily see the emotions playing across his face. Disbelief to amazement to...

"Okay, Richard. I'm ready for you to help me." Debbie glanced at the floor. It was all she could do to keep her feet from sliding toward the hole in the center of the tower.

"I don't think so. Good luck, ladies," he said coolly, saluting with his free hand as he retreated into the shadows of the stairwell.

"He's leaving us!" Janet cried, her cheeks pink with anger. "I'll try 911 again." She reached for her phone with shaky hands and tapped the screen a few times.

Suddenly, the phone tumbled from her grasp and through the hole in the floor.

"No!" they cried out in unison.

Debbie pulled out her phone and tapped the screen. Nothing. She had forgotten to charge it the previous night.

"Let me guess—your phone is dead." Janet brushed a strand of hair from her forehead.

"Yeah. I did arrange to meet here with Greg though. He said he would come as soon as he could. He's probably already on his way from another worksite." She slid her phone back into her pocket, fully aware of Janet's pinched expression.

"Why don't we try to move around the sides toward the door, but in opposite directions?" Janet suggested, her voice trembling.

Debbie tried, but the floor gave a threatening creak beneath her foot before she even put weight on it.

Janet crept closer to the stairs. Another board cracked beneath her weight, and she pressed herself flat against the wall again.

"We might be here for a while," Debbie said.

Janet sighed. "I hope not. I'm not sure the floor will hold out much longer."

Debbie blew out a harsh breath, refusing to let panic settle in. To distract herself, she chose to focus on the mystery. "Who would have ever thought that the loot from the train was historical documents?" she said.

"Dennison has kept rumors of the treasure alive for years, but everyone assumed it would be a bag full of banknotes. Not George Washington's inaugural speech. Wouldn't the powers that be know these were missing from the Library of Congress and come searching for them?" Janet moved again, skipping the board that had protested.

"If we ever get out of here, you and I will make some calls. Hey, be careful!" Debbie yelled as the board beneath Janet's foot dipped downward.

Janet halted. "Debbie, I don't want us to fall."

"We won't," Debbie soothed, wishing she could hold her friend's hand and offer some comfort. A shudder rippled through her. She pushed aside the mental picture of a shattered phone scattered across the hardwood floor below. "Keep talking. Believe me, it works. Beatrice kept me distracted when I crawled into the icehouse."

A loud sigh escaped from Janet as she clung to the wall. "I have a bad feeling about all of this. Ian doesn't know where I am. Richard will likely lie to Beatrice about us, and—"

"Stop," Debbie ordered firmly. "We just need to hang on a little longer." She kept her quivering legs flat against the wall just inches from where the floor dipped downward like a slide at an amusement park.

For one long moment neither of them said another word— which was even more dreadful.

Janet's next question brought a welcome relief. "You'd think a huge robbery of our country's most important documents would be all over the national news, wouldn't you?"

Debbie raised an eyebrow. "Maybe not with Nazi spies infiltrating the country. Remember, we've encountered similar cases. Nazis tried to blow up train stations and factories—thankfully, to no avail. I think Myrtle wanted to thwart something. Otherwise, she could have taken the documents straight to Germany with the red carpet rolled out for her. The question is, why did she hide them?"

"Because the other men with her wanted them."

"Yes. Somehow the Black Cat evaded her colleagues and hid the documents so they could never be found. What better place than a church?"

"With a school poem to guide her son," Janet said.

"Remember the other poem she quoted? The one about the captain of her soul? No crook would quote that poem. She wanted to reassure her son of something. A change of heart, maybe?"

"I wonder who or what changed her mind? According to that article in your purse, she was perhaps one of America's most successful female thieves."

"I think it was her son. Julia, her granddaughter, told me that Walter fought overseas. How could Myrtle betray her country and her son? Especially when the newspapers plastered her face everywhere because of her escape from prison. She went to a lot of trouble to make sure her son knew the truth about her."

"But then she disappeared. For good. What happened?"

Debbie didn't want to answer what she feared most. Someone must have gotten to Myrtle Cooper, but who? And what end had it brought her?

A wild gust of wind sent a shudder rippling through the tower, and Debbie had to wonder if she and her best friend faced their own end.

CHAPTER TWENTY-FIVE

Columbus, Ohio
April 16, 1942

Jack dialed his superior one last time before he caught the next train. He was so close, he could nearly taste it. He would hunt down the missing documents and every last thief, and when he did, someone would pay the price.

"Did you find her?" his superior demanded.

Jack evaded the question as he eyed the train platform. "My agents continue to comb the area for Gavin Schroeder. The man we captured—Jimmy—knows about each secret hideout used by his gang. We'll flush out the others one way or another."

He braced himself for a fiery lecture from the other end of the phone. Good thing he was thousands of miles from Washington, or his ears would be scorched by now.

"How will you cover your tracks, Lund?"

Jack pinched the bridge of his nose as he stood in the hotel hallway. "We've kept the heist contained to a couple of local newspapers. We've ensured the story won't get out."

"It better not. I won't tolerate mistakes. Neither will Mother."

Jack swallowed a groan. No one wanted to anger the president. It tended to have a dampening effect on one's career. Perhaps now wasn't the best moment to share the rest of his plan.

The Black Cat had covered her tracks well, darting from town to town, always under a different disguise. But he had finally stumbled across a useful lead.

"Try Mexico," Jimmy had said. "Gavin mentioned that she'd head south, where no one would know her name or her face."

So Jack plastered pictures of her in every newspaper one more time, feeding the story of the escaped convict when it should have died.

Finally, a few calls had trickled in. Mimi, or Myrtle, or whatever her name was, had left a trail. He was good at tracking. It was just a matter of time.

CHAPTER TWENTY-SIX

Thirty minutes passed while Debbie and Janet racked their brains to figure out how to escape the crumbling belfry. Shouting hadn't done any good, and Debbie's throat felt raw.

She wasn't sure how much longer she could cling to the wall. "I'm taking a mini vacation when this is finished," she said as she wiggled her toes in her flats. "I feel so bad. I've been promising Greg an evening or afternoon, and it's just not working out this month. We went out for a quick bite a few nights ago, but I need to take some real quality time for him."

"You should slow down and enjoy life. Don't let him slip through your fingers. He's a keeper," Janet advised, her gaze warm and understanding.

"Everyone else seems to think so. Including Gloria."

Janet narrowed her eyes at the name. "I can't believe she tried to set you up for the theft of the bunny suit. As punishment, I think she should have to wear it in the parade."

Debbie laughed weakly. "Sounds fair." But the laughter caused her to slide forward until she frantically clutched at the wainscoting, her fingers cramped from the effort.

"Debbie!" Janet cried.

Down below, someone else shouted her name. Her noisy breathing hushed as she strained to hear whoever was below them.

"Debbie! Where are you?"

She knew that voice.

She yelled back, "Greg! We're in the tower, and there's an enormous hole in the floor. We're trapped!"

Dimly, she heard him say something she couldn't quite make out. He sounded irritated.

"Be careful coming up the stairs. They're not stable," Janet yelled.

Footsteps, careful and measured, climbed higher and higher until, at last, Greg's rugged form filled the narrow doorway. Debbie thought she had never seen a better sight.

He took in their locations and the gaping hole. His Adam's apple bobbed, but his tone was even when he spoke. "I'm going to hold out my arm to you, and I want you to slide toward me as if you're on thin ice. Keep your weight as even as you can with each step. If the floor makes a sound, jump to me. I'll catch you."

"Take Janet first. She's closer to you," Debbie insisted.

He shot Debbie a long, unreadable look. For a moment, she thought he might argue with her, or worse, chastise her for going into a building in desperate need of repairs without waiting for him. Blowing out a harsh breath, he said, "All right. Janet, you first."

Janet obeyed, creeping slowly until she could leap to him. He pulled her into the stairwell with a grunt.

"Can you get Debbie across safely?" Janet sounded winded, but she was safe.

When Greg faced Debbie, a frown creased his tanned forehead. With one arm, he grabbed the doorframe for balance and reached out for her with the other. "Come on."

"I don't think I can move another inch without the floor collapsing," she whispered.

"You can," he urged, his eyes never leaving hers. "I won't let you fall, Debbie."

Gulping, she crept forward, ignoring the threatening sounds of the rotten floor. She clung to the wood trim lining the walls as she went. It wasn't much, but it brought a small sense of security, as did Greg's open hand, reaching for hers.

He tipped forward, bracing his work boots against the doorway, and their fingertips brushed.

Suddenly the floor fell away beneath her, and she screamed.

Greg's strong fingers wrapped around her wrist as wood and dust and plaster rained down on the lower floors. For a moment, she couldn't tear her gaze away from his white face, the strain of his neck, and the muscles lining his arm as he hauled her to safety.

When she stood on the stairwell, her legs buckled.

He caught her and scooped her up. "Hang on, Debbie."

"You're not going to carry me all the way down the stairs," she protested weakly.

A teasing glint shone in his eyes. "I don't think I have much choice. You're exhausted."

When the three of them reached the sanctuary, he set her on her feet. Debbie knew she ought to head outside, but for some reason, she couldn't budge. Not with her legs shaking.

Greg did not remove his arm from around her waist.

"I was afraid you wouldn't make it here in time," she told him.

"I got sidetracked at my other worksite, but when I realized I was late, I came as fast as I could. Besides, I need to talk to you about Gloria." He paused, his expression almost tentative. "I'm not interested in her, no matter what games she's playing. I'm only interested in one woman—you."

"You might be a knight in shining armor." She smiled up at him despite the wobbly feeling in her knees. "To Janet too."

To her surprise, he bent his head and brushed his warm lips against hers, the kiss as sweet as could be.

He folded her in a tight hug, his scent of woodsy spice clinging to her. "I'm glad I found you both before anyone could get hurt."

Debbie got out of Greg's truck when he parked at Beatrice's house. With Washington's inaugural speech tucked in her jacket, no less. She pulled it out to study it one more time while Greg called Ian about Richard.

Greg hung up then leaned over to read the elegant script. "Wow. This is…"

"Surreal," she supplied for him when he couldn't finish the thought.

Janet parked behind Greg's truck and joined them. Together, they approached the front porch.

"Ian's hunting for Richard right now," Janet informed them. "He's also set up a perimeter around town in case Richard tries to bolt."

To Debbie's relief, she saw a patrol car coming down the street toward Morrow House. Maybe Ian would bring good news regarding Richard's capture.

Debbie knocked on the door.

Beatrice opened it, her eyes red. "I'm so glad to see you, Debbie. Please, come inside. Bring your friends."

Debbie hugged her former teacher. "I've got some interesting news for you, Beatrice."

"Me too, honey. Me too." Beatrice glanced over Debbie's shoulder. "I'm so glad to see Janet's husband."

A familiar figure waited in the parlor, dressed in ivory from head to toe. Cecilia Belanger, the appraiser and antique dealer. She rose from the couch, her expression sorrowful. "I'm afraid I haven't made the best impression on you, Debbie. I'm so sorry." She held out her hand, gold bracelets tinkling on her wrist. "I'm a hunter of rare antiques with unusual histories. I thought Beatrice was genuinely interested in selling to me at first. After all, I'd been told about a magnificent strand of pearls with a possible link to the train robbery of 1942. Unfortunately, I've had sellers insist they wanted nothing to do with me solely to drive up their price. I thought Beatrice was playing a similar game."

She pulled a velvet box from her coat pocket and opened it, revealing a gleaming row of pearls the color of midnight. The very pearls Debbie had touched and lost.

There was a knock at the door, and Beatrice let Ian into the house, his expression neutral as he strode to his wife's side.

Cecilia's gaze flickered to the police uniform, and she cleared her throat loudly. "I wanted the necklace more than I've ever wanted anything in my professional career. I may be ruthless, but I'm not a thief. Vicky, Beatrice's assistant, offered me the necklace and told me Beatrice had changed her mind."

Debbie inhaled sharply.

Cecelia nodded to her. "I was surprised too. Unnerved, even. But Richard called me and corroborated her story that Beatrice had agreed to the sale. He even produced a handwritten note stating the necklace was to be his as an inheritance. I tried to call Beatrice to confirm, but the call would go right to voice mail, so I wondered if her phone was off or if she had blocked my number. I came to confront Richard, but instead I found Vicky here. When she brought out the necklace and demanded payment, I asked her if she and Richard had stolen it from Beatrice. Vicky just turned around and ran, leaving the pearls behind. I called the police right away."

"I tried to call you, Debbie, but your phone must have died," Beatrice added, hiccupping as more tears filled her eyes. "I'm so sorry about my nephew's behavior. I love him, but he has to be held accountable for his actions."

Debbie put her arm around Beatrice's shoulders. "I can't tell you how relieved I am that you have your pearls back. Vicky must have stolen them the night I hosted the Easter planning meeting at my house."

"I agree," Ian said. "It wouldn't have been hard to take them during the meeting with so many people there."

"So you didn't crawl into the icehouse?" Debbie asked Cecelia. "We found an ivory button in there that we thought might have come from you."

"That was Vicky. I found her muddy shirt in the garbage," Beatrice said. "She and Richard were working together."

Debbie frowned at the news. No wonder Beatrice appeared so crestfallen. "I'm so sorry. Where are they now?"

"They've been caught outside Dennison," Ian announced. "Both of them fell all over themselves throwing each other under the bus. We've also recovered the rest of the materials they stole."

Debbie exhaled with relief. She no longer had a reason to hide her latest find. "Good. Because Richard didn't get everything." She removed the crumpled papers from her jacket and showed them to Beatrice, Cecilia, and Ian. The room grew silent as Ian took the document.

The tall police officer appeared completely unsettled. "I don't know what to say." His Scottish brogue deepened. "My wife and her best friend discovered George Washington's inauguration speech, as well as the other documents Richard had." He stared at his wife.

Janet merely grinned and waggled her eyebrows.

"May I?" Cecilia held out her hand to take the document. Ian offered it to her. She studied the papers for several minutes, her lips moving as she silently read. Then she raised her head, her eyes glowing. "Did you ever hear the tale of the government hiding key documents around the country during World War II?"

Heeding Cecilia's advice, Debbie called the Library of Congress. The conversation would be burned into her memory for the rest of her life.

Everyone listened as she described what she had found. Beatrice took photos of the documents while a kind librarian at the Library of Congress answered Debbie's questions.

Debbie eventually ended the call, her mind struggling to process the information she'd learned.

Janet nudged her. "What did they say?"

"Cecilia is right. Federal agents removed documents from the Library after the Japanese struck Pearl Harbor. The president expressed concern about the safety of Washington and the immense history preserved there. Important documents were sent by train to several secret locations, including Fort Knox, which is virtually impenetrable."

"Fort Knox holds the gold reserves," Greg said.

"Right," Debbie said. "Back then, no one knew what to expect from the Germans. Everything of value had to be secured. The woman said that the government feared Nazi spies finding the documents and stealing them. Perhaps to shame the United States and demoralize us, or to demand ransom."

Janet folded her arms across her middle. "Imagine the damage the wrong person could have done if they had gotten away with the documents. But why didn't anyone ever recover these?"

"The Secret Service sent out fake documents like these to trap thieves."

"They're fake?" Janet said. "Wow. I never would have guessed."

"It makes sense. I wondered why the story never made the national news. The government didn't want anyone to get wind of their plot to ferret out spies. Only the president of the United States, the Library of Congress, and a handful of agents knew about the fakes."

"Incredible," Cecilia murmured. "I wonder if Myrtle Cooper knew she had stolen something that was supposed to help capture her?"

Debbie thought of the photograph of the woman Beatrice's mother had known as Myrtle Cooper. A mysterious woman, right to the end. "I'm not sure we'll ever discover what happened to her. She truly disappeared. But I'd like to think she reformed at the end."

"I wonder who, or what, would have influenced her to?" Janet asked as she reached for her husband's hand.

Debbie found her gaze sliding to meet Greg's, and she smiled. "I bet it was someone who believed in her."

CHAPTER TWENTY-SEVEN

Granbury, Texas
April 20, 1942

The station was crowded when Myrtle stepped off the train. Texas presented a vastly different vista from Ohio, but she recognized a small town when she saw one. Women strode past her, wearing cotton dresses, thanks to the warmer temperatures. Winter down south presented opposites. Greener grass. The sense of impending spring and summer melded together. The sun gleamed warm and bright. She touched her hair—now a deep auburn and nothing like the lackluster brown or platinum blond of her past.

"Hide in plain sight," Arnold had told her. As soon as she left Ohio, she'd stopped at a secondhand store for an assortment of skirts and blouses. The money the Armstrongs had given her wouldn't last long, but she felt if she could make it to Texas, close enough to flee to Mexico, she'd be safe. Maybe she could find a sleepy village and work as a waitress or something.

She no longer resembled either the dashing Mimi Jarman or the plain Myrtle Cooper. Her white blouse, black skirt, and simple heels garnered no attention, although maybe her hair color did. When she'd wired her messages from the border town of Harlingen to the Plain Dealer, no one recognized her or questioned her. At least Walter would know she was alive.

Her stomach rumbled, so she found a nearby café serving hot coffee and sandwiches. She skipped the coffee and purchased a snack for the road. Meanwhile, her gaze snagged on the newspaper stand positioned right outside the café window.

Unable to help herself, she skimmed the headlines. Her shoulders slumped when she saw her face on the front page again, with the obligatory "WHERE IS THE BLACK CAT?"

The headline competed with news about the war. She should have been connected to the train robbery, but nothing she'd seen in the past three months suggested she'd played a role in the Dennison fiasco. Even her escape story had been relegated to the less important sections of the newspaper, without a single hint about trains or Gavin Schroeder.

Why wouldn't the robbery make national news? She had held George Washington's handwritten inaugural speech, Thomas Jefferson's diary entries, and Abraham Lincoln's letters to his wife in her shaking hands.

The hairs on the back of her neck rose, thanks to a sixth sense honed by tasting far too much danger. Slowly, she raised her head. Her vivid reflection stared at her through the window glass. Hard features. Unfamiliar with auburn hair and no makeup. But that wasn't what made her flinch.

The familiar shape of a man stood in the narrow alley. He watched her with a knowing smirk.

Waiting for her.

CHAPTER TWENTY-EIGHT

The late Easter celebration fell on a beautiful day at the end of April. The parade and egg hunt proved a great success, with colorful eggs scattered across the lush green lawn of McCluskey Park. Debbie watched as children raced through the grass with baskets, snatching the brightly colored eggs hidden behind trees and park benches. Laughter filled the cool air.

Rose wore the ridiculous bunny suit, waving to the children who ran up to her with their filled baskets.

Debbie hid a chuckle. Gloria had apologized—albeit unconvincingly—and Greg had set the record straight, telling her he wasn't interested in a relationship with her. Not when he had a crush on one of the owners of the Whistle Stop Café.

Greg nudged her shoulder with his. "This is quite a date, Debbie."

She laughed. She and Greg had ridden in a pale blue 1942 convertible covered in balloons for the chamber of commerce entry. They'd tossed candy to kids lining the curbs. Sometimes the simplest solution really was the best. Greg had put his foot down on an elaborate float.

Near the beginning of the parade, Greg had intertwined his fingers with hers, declaring to all of Dennison that things were real between them. He still held her hand now, while Janet and Ian joined in the fun with Greg's sons, Jaxon and Julian, who helped the younger kids find some of the more well-hidden eggs.

Debbie had been pleased when Beatrice joined the festivities. Although she appeared tired, a smile lit her face as she approached Debbie. "You couldn't have planned a better event, Debbie. Everyone is asking if you'll do it again next year."

Debbie held up a palm. "Not a chance. This is my one and only contribution to the Easter celebration. It's been quite an adventure, but I'm more than happy to pass the baton to the next leader. I'm ready for a break. I'm going to slow down my life, especially since the tourist season will pick up soon for summer."

"Smart girl. It's good to say no, isn't it? I'm learning the same lesson, albeit later in life."

"A worthy lesson," Debbie murmured.

Beatrice sucked in a deep breath. "I won't keep you, but I wanted you to know that I'm sending the pearls to Myrtle's granddaughter. I think she should have one keepsake from the grandmother she never met. Did you ever solve her story?"

Debbie sighed. "No. I searched online again last night, but I can't find anything about her. I'd like to think she found redemption at the end of her life."

Beatrice stuffed her hands into her coat pockets. "I agree. No one quotes 'Captain of My Soul' without a reason. Perhaps Esmé and Pastor Darrel had more influence than we'll ever know. I've also been mulling over how to use my home, especially now that Vicky and Richard are no longer with me. At first I thought about a bed-and-breakfast, but Dennison doesn't need another one of those.

Then I realized that perhaps I should take a page out of my grand-mother's book. Why not open it to women in need? I've got plenty of rooms. Maybe I can round up the funding to repair the conserva-tory, the extra bedrooms, and the attic, and make the house useful again."

"I love that idea," Debbie said. She almost volunteered to help, especially with such a worthy cause, before she remembered her commitment to slowing down. To pray about when she ought to say yes and when to say no.

"I've got Ian and Janet on board. Kim Smith too. You take a break, Debbie," Beatrice said with a knowing twinkle in her eyes.

"Thank you," Debbie said. "I'll let you know if and when I can commit to helping."

When Beatrice was drawn into another conversation, Greg led Debbie toward a bench. Together, they sat down, enjoying the bright sunshine and the peaceful moment. She waved to Jaxon and Julian. Later, she and Greg would take them out for dinner.

"I'm sorry you haven't found out what you want to know about Myrtle." Greg looped his arm around her shoulders. The weight of his arm felt wonderful—warm and secure.

"I just wish I knew what happened to her," Debbie said. "I'd like to think she wasn't killed by her cohorts or that she didn't die in prison."

"Perhaps some things are meant to remain a mystery," he said. "At least her family will have peace that Myrtle didn't steal the coun-try's treasures. She might have even given her life believing that she was protecting our history. I bet she did it for her son."

Debbie didn't have all the answers, but as she sat beside Greg, she realized he was right. Myrtle's story had unfolded in the manner it ought—providing enough closure for two families. One day, the truth would be fully revealed. Meanwhile, she was going to enjoy this beautiful day with a good man.

She had been immeasurably blessed with her family, friends, and now Greg.

It was enough. It was more than enough.

CHAPTER TWENTY-NINE

She could never hide. Her heart hammering in her chest, Myrtle dashed onto the train. He had seen her, tipping his fedora in salute.

Suddenly, the pieces fell into place as she found her seat. How on earth would she hide? She couldn't stop the moving train and escape into the countryside. Her breathing quickened as she glanced frantically about for an escape. She could practically hear Arthur's voice lecturing her. She'd definitely lost her edge, panicking and trapping herself as she hadn't done since her training days.

Confident in his capture, the man sauntered down the narrow aisle and sank into the velvet seat across from hers. "You're quite a difficult woman to find, Mrs. Jarman."

She forced her features into the familiar smooth planes, ideally devoid of emotion even as her pulse raced at the thought of returning to prison. "And yet, here you are."

He smiled and folded one trousered leg over the other while tapping his long fingers against the armrest of the seat. Elegant. The picture of ease. Not too handsome, but nothing to sneer at either. "I mustn't forget my manners. I'm Jack Lund, with the Secret Service."

She eyed him, and he her, their mutual gazes probing for any weakness. Finally, a resigned sigh escaped her. "Okay, you win. The jig is up. Go ahead and flash your badge and handcuffs. I won't fight."

"No?" He tilted his head. "Because you seem like a fighter, and I would much prefer a warrior to a meek little mouse."

Her careful mask nearly slipped. What was he talking about?

He leaned forward. "I will not arrest you."

Unease rippled through her. He must be like the other corrupt business owners and politicians she'd had the misfortune of crossing. He would offer her a *bribe for the location of the documents and then likely dispose of her body.*

As if reading her thoughts, he held up a hand. "But I'd like to know where the documents are hidden. I know you got close to Esmé Morrow and Pastor Darrel Armstrong. I'd really hate to involve them any further."

She didn't want anyone else to get hurt. Especially people who had been so kind to her.

"Are they at Morrow House or the church?"

She must have flinched, since his smile deepened.

"The church, I'll wager," he said. "Good. I suspected as much. I plan to leave the package right where you placed it."

"Why?" Her eyebrows shot upward at the surprising revelation.

"Because I think your associate, Gavin, has some ties we're interested in. If they come hunting for those documents, we'll be waiting for them and nab them in the act."

We'll be waiting. Her mouth dried. She shifted on the cushioned seat when he steepled his fingers together, his gaze sharpening. Gavin was still on the loose—a horrible thought.

"I'm offering you a job, Mrs. Jarman. In case you haven't noticed, we have a war on our hands, one that has reached our shores with Nazi and Japanese spies.

I need a woman who can pull off designer shoes or a pair of muddy boots. One with the guts to scale a prison wall and take down our enemies with her bare hands."

She could hardly believe what she was hearing. He was offering her a legitimate job, using skills she already had? But she was a notorious criminal with a sentence of nearly a hundred years—probably more since her escape.

"You're joking."

He folded his arms across his chest. "I don't joke about things that matter. Certainly not about someone I need to be able to trust with my life. I select my subordinates with the greatest of care, and I reject about thirty men every single quarter."

She sucked in a deep breath, her mind whirling. "How can you trust me? I'm a convict."

"A convict headed to Washington, yes? In case you haven't noticed, this is a northbound train."

His abrupt question startled her into silence.

"You're not crossing the border," he said. "You're headed in the wrong direction, and I think I understand you well enough by now to know that you didn't get on this train by mistake."

"I changed my mind," she whispered, staring down at her hands. Would he understand Walter's plea for her to make the right choices?

"Surrendering to the authorities?"

She bit the inside of her cheek. She had decided never to run again. If that meant spending the rest of her days behind bars—well, for Walter's sake, she would do it.

The agent continued to watch her. "If you sign with me, you'll get a full pardon. It's not a game. It'll be hard, dangerous work. But you're used to that, aren't you?"

"Yes, I am," she murmured as she readjusted her gloves, the action soothing against the shock building inside of her. "Do you need me to sign a contract or something?"

"After you hear my conditions. I haven't told you the hardest part yet. You'll never talk to your son again. Everyone thinks you're dead or on the run—a corrupt woman likely headed for the beaches south of the border. I need them to continue to believe that. Both Myrtle and Mimi need to be dead to the world. Your task will be to escort documents to Fort Knox. One day, you'll retrieve them and return them to the Library of Congress. But for now, I need you to lure Gavin back into the open. I just found out last month that the documents you stole were fakes designed to serve as bait. Now I'm going to use them to ferret out Nazis. So you will never contact your boy again. Not if you truly care about his life."

She had instinctively known that the last time she'd talked to Walter, months ago, was truly the last time she ever would. But hearing Jack say it in so many words felt like a punch square to her gut. She blinked several times and twisted to look out the window so he wouldn't see her tears.

After she composed herself and faced him again, she found that compassion warmed his icy blue eyes.

"While your son is fighting on the front lines, you'll be fighting the enemy from within. Who knows how many innocent boys, how many sons you might save in the end?" Jack's voice was soft.

Her mama had once told her that she could fly on the wings of eagles. She would run and not grow weary. She would not faint if she stayed in the shelter of God's plan. And though Mama would hate to see what had happened to her daughter's life, Myrtle recalled Pastor Darrel's words as he'd driven her out of Dennison. "It's not too late for redemption. It's never too late to start again, despite the previous ruin and ashes."

Perhaps she had been made for such a time as this. Perhaps God could use her skills for something far better than she could have ever imagined.

"I'll do it, Mr. Lund." She nodded, though her heart broke at the idea of losing her boy. But true love meant *sacrifice, and she would do anything to protect him. To one day make him proud of her.*

Jack's smile returned. "Welcome to the Secret Service, Myrtle."

As the train rattled down the tracks and the countryside passed in a blur, her path remained unknown but not without a flicker of hope. She had planned to fade away into some remote Mexican town, spending the rest of her days cooking in a greasy diner. Then she had planned to throw herself on whatever mercy the justice system might have for her.

Apparently, God had other ideas.

Perhaps there were a few more lives left in the Black Cat. It was time to rise again.

Dear Reader,

I hope you enjoyed Debbie and Janet's latest adventure.

Myrtle's story and the transportation of precious documents are based on true stories. Most Americans never knew about the secret transfer of the documents to prevent ransom or theft, but during the war, the Founding Father letters, the Magna Carta, and other priceless artifacts and art were moved via train to Fort Knox and other underground bunkers throughout the United States. After the war, agents escorted each item back to the Library of Congress. And it all occurred right under our noses.

My editors asked for a train robbery story. I hunted for weeks, searching historical records for one measly attempt. As far as I could find, *no one* successfully robbed a train during WWII. No one, to my knowledge, was foolish enough to try to rob a train full of soldiers. However, when I stumbled across Eleanor Jarman's story, the woman Myrtle is based on, I knew I had found my master thief. When I learned about the secret transport of documents via train, I knew I had my mystery.

How much of Myrtle's story is based on real life? Convicted of murder—although she wasn't the one to pull the trigger—Eleanor was sent to a federal prison with a sentence of 199 years. After hearing that her son was about to run away from her sister's home, she scaled a prison wall and went to check on her children. She disappeared after that, and the newspapers were on fire with the whereabouts of "the Blonde Tigress." She was never a federal agent, but she did send coded messages to her family through the classifieds. I decided to give Eleanor a happy ending and redemption as Myrtle. After all, she certainly had the gumption to be an agent.

Did women take part in the clandestine and demonstrate feats of incredible physical endurance during the Second World War? I'm happy to report that they did! My inspiration for Myrtle also came from the infamous Russian, Lyudmila Pavlichenko, aka Lady Death, who was the deadliest female sniper in history. The Germans so feared her, they attempted to bribe her to join their army. Not even the best German snipers could match her skill and steely resolve.

Nancy Wake, originally from New Zealand, was another such woman. Known as the White Mouse, she found her calling as a French resistance leader. She risked her life to help Jews and Allied soldiers escape the Germans on dangerous routes through France. She had an exorbitant bounty on her head and lost her husband to the Nazis, but she never gave up. She lived to a ripe old age, with adventure and tales worthy of the movie screen.

The stories of World War II are filled with women pushed to their very limits and achieving great things at great cost.

All of these stories remind us—*never underestimate a woman.*

Until next time,
Jenelle Hovde

ABOUT the AUTHOR

Jenelle Hovde writes biblical historical fiction and cozy mysteries. When she isn't scribbling on scraps of paper, you can find her in used bookstores perusing antique romance novels and historical journals. You also might find her at the beach with a favorite read.

TRUTH BEHIND the FICTION

The Transportation of Secret Documents

ere weeks after the attack on Pearl Harbor, a secretive mission took place on American soil. The men in charge were the head librarian of the Library of Congress, Archibald MacLeish, and Secret Service agent Harry Neal. The Library of Congress and the president agreed to relocate important documents, national treasures, and the Magna Carta, which was on loan from the British for safekeeping due to the Nazi invasions. The treasures were transported in simple wooden crates to mysterious locations throughout the United States.

Routes were established from the Library of Congress to Union Station, with undercover agents escorting the boxes. Travelers had no reason to suspect the agents or the contents of the crates traveling via train.

What treasures were whisked away to underground bunkers? They included the Gutenberg Bible, the Articles of Confederation, Lincoln's second inaugural address and Gettysburg Address, the Constitution of the United States, and the Declaration of Independence. Precious art, Mary Todd Lincoln's pearls, presidential diaries including George Washington's memories, and many other priceless documents tied to our country's history were also hidden away. After the war, agents returned every item with the exception of two notebooks belonging to the American poet, Walt Whitman. One of them is still unaccounted for.

Fort Knox offered the perfect, impenetrable location. It provided protection against Nazi spies or bomb threats due to its location in Louisville, Kentucky, far from the coast.

The threat of enemy sabotage was real. During the war, Nazi infiltrators were arrested on American soil with plans to disable factories and train stations. Americans did their due diligence to keep their country safe. Fires, bombs, and sabotage had to be averted, or the history of American freedom would be lost forever, just like the ill-fated library of ancient Alexandria.

Before the US entered the war, seven hundred vetted volunteers catalogued and packed five thousand boxes, so all MacLeish had to do was move them to shelters that were waterproof, bombproof, and climate-controlled. They scouted out thirty other locations in Virginia, West Virginia, and Kentucky, but selected only three. Eventually, they added another location in Ohio.

Artworks by Botticelli, Raphael, Titian, Donatello, Goya, and Rembrandt were packed away to Biltmore House. The women and men who traveled the rails with them, intent on their everyday lives, never knew their luggage brushed against greatness.

Had the Declaration of Independence or the Constitution been stolen or destroyed, the effect would have been devastating for American morale. The agents who guarded the treasures put their lives on the line to ensure America's recorded history would be preserved for future generations.

FROM the HOME-FRONT KITCHEN

Water Pie

Water pie is a fabulous Great Depression recipe consisting of the simplest and most affordable ingredients to make a swoon-worthy caramelized custard.

Ingredients:

1 9-inch deep-dish piecrust, unbaked

1½ cups water OR 1 can lemon-lime soda

1 cup sugar, regular or powdered

¼ cup flour

2 teaspoons vanilla extract

5 tablespoons butter, cut into 5 pieces

1 teaspoon cinnamon (optional)

Directions:

Preheat oven to 400 degrees.

Place unbaked piecrust into a deep-dish pie pan, fold and trim edges. Pour water or soda into piecrust.

In small bowl, stir together flour and sugar.

Sprinkle flour mixture over water. Do not stir.

Drizzle vanilla over mixture. Do not stir.

Place pats of butter on top of the mixture. Do not stir. The butter will melt evenly into the mixture as the pie bakes.

Sprinkle with cinnamon if desired.

Bake pie at 400 degrees for 30 minutes. Reduce temperature to 375 degrees and cover edges of crust with foil to prevent burning. Bake for an additional 30 minutes.

Allow pie to cool completely (it will be watery at first) and then refrigerate for several hours before cutting. You should see a golden crust, and filling with the consistency of a custard once fully cooled.

Voilà! Your pie is now ready to eat. Serve with whipped cream or ice cream.

*Read on for a sneak peek of another exciting book
in the* Whistle Stop Café Mysteries *series!*

SOMEWHERE OVER THE RAINBOW

BY LAURA BRADFORD

*J*anet Shaw moved between tables with a lightness that had nothing to do with the lilac-scented May air wafting through the open café windows or the high praise her new peach pie had earned from her regulars. No, this lightness, this joy, was about something a million times better. Something she'd been waiting for since mid-January when—

"Oh." Janet stopped, gazed over a customer's shoulder, and took in the sketch gracing the bottom two-thirds of a napkin that bore the café's logo. "Did you draw that?"

The gray-haired newcomer set her pencil down and pushed the napkin into the center of the table. "I did, but it's nothing. Just a house I glimpsed through some trees the other day. It was a fast glance, though, so I improvised a lot. And not terribly well, I'm afraid."

Janet took in the cottage-like house, the flowers lining what appeared to be a slate walkway, and the pair of cozy rockers on the front porch that made her yearn to sit in one and watch the day go by. "Are you kidding me? It's *beautiful*. How long have you been drawing like that?"

"If my mother were still alive, she'd say that I've spent far too much of my life doodling on paper, napkins, sticky notes, and anything else I could find. But my fingers can't seem to stop themselves sometimes. It's what I do. What I've always done."

Janet stepped around the side of the table to speak with the woman more easily. "I've been doodling my whole life. And that"—Janet indicated the napkin—"is most definitely not doodling."

"You're too kind." The woman pointed at her empty plate and then smiled up at Janet. "I have to say, that chocolate cream pie might very well be the best I've ever had. And I've had a lot over the years. Is it exclusively a Saturday offering?"

"I'm glad you enjoyed it, and no, it's a regular on our menu."

"Good to know." The woman's gaze dropped from Janet's. "I like your shirt."

Janet looked down at the bold white lettering that ran across her chest—I Bake, Therefore I Am—and laughed. Usually, her punny T-shirts were covered by her apron, but this was a special one she'd wanted to show off to the café crowd. "Thank you. My daughter, Tiffany, found it for me in a shop not far from her college and gave it to me last night."

Then, unable to hold back her happiness, Janet lowered herself onto the edge of the vacant chair across from the woman. "She officially completed her first year at Case Western Reserve University in Cleveland yesterday, and I'm beyond thrilled at having her home with me for the entire summer. When she's not working or hanging out with her friends, that is."

"I see. The humming makes sense now."

"I was humming?" Janet asked.

The woman nodded, smiling. "Your girl is back in the nest again. It makes sense."

"Back in the nest. I like that." Janet extended her hand to the woman with a grin. "I'm Janet Shaw. My friend Debbie Albright and I own this café."

"I'm Audrey Barker, Dennison's newest resident, according to my real estate agent."

"How wonderful. Welcome! You're going to love it here—I just know it."

"That's music to my ears. Thank you."

"What brings you to Dennison?" Janet asked. "Do you have family here?"

Audrey's smile dimmed momentarily. "No, I'm the last of the Barkers, I'm afraid. But I needed to downsize, and I wanted to stay in Ohio. When I did a little research on towns in this county, Dennison really stood out to me."

"I take it you're a history buff?" Janet prodded.

"I don't know if I qualify as a history buff, per se, but Dennison's—and this depot's—ties to World War II intrigue me." Audrey ran the tip of her index finger around her empty coffee mug. "My father often spoke about coming through this depot on his way to war. He talked of the townspeople and the kindness they showed him and the other soldiers."

"That's wonderful," Janet said. "When you have time, I highly encourage you to check out the museum at the other end of the building. Kim Smith, the curator, has a wealth of information regarding the station and the service members it served. In fact, Kim's mother, Eileen Palmer, actually stepped in as stationmaster during the Second World War and is still living right here in Dennison."

Audrey leaned forward, intrigued. "How fascinating."

"It truly is. Kim does an amazing job making history come to life for visitors," Janet said. "I could go on and on, but suffice it to say that you've picked a wonderful place to call home, Audrey. The kindness your father spoke about is still very much alive and well in this town. It really is."

"And a person can get a *very* nice piece of chocolate cream pie here every day of the week," Audrey said with a chuckle.

"Every day but Sunday," Janet corrected.

"Of course. Sunday is the Lord's Day." Audrey tapped her empty plate. "But knowing it's here the other six days of the week will be a nice carrot—and, at times, a solace—as I get settled in my new home."

Janet crossed one leg over the other. "What do you need a carrot for?"

"I engaged in far too much procrastination in the weeks leading up to my move. As a result, the failure to pare down my belongings before I got here has resulted in the need for a storage unit I'd rather not continue to pay for. Thus, your pie will serve as my carrot to finally go through everything once and for all. I'll allow myself a piece only on days that I've made some progress emptying the unit."

"And the solace?"

Audrey's eyes filled with tears. "Much of what's in that storage unit belonged to my mom. She passed two years ago at the age of ninety-seven."

"I'm sorry for your loss."

"Thank you," Audrey said, recovering. "I'll be donating most of her books to the local library and her clothes to any women's shelters in the area, but I need to go through the rest of her things and decide what to keep."

"Naturally. It's good that you have a plan."

"Yes, that helps, but the whole task still feels overwhelming. Makes me wish I had a fairy godmother who could drop down from the sky and do all the sorting for me." Audrey stretched, and kneaded her lower back. "If left to my own devices, I'll hem and haw over every little item, no matter how inconsequential it might be."

Janet considered the woman's words. "I'm sure you could probably find someone to do that for you. Maybe a college kid home for…" The words faded from her lips as her thoughts caught up to her mouth.

"Is your daughter looking for work?" Audrey asked, her eyes widening. "Because I'll pay, and I'll pay well if she is."

"Actually, she's fairly free right now," Janet said. "She has a standing job as a lifeguard every summer, starting in June. And the only thing I need her for is to help me plan her father's birthday party at the end of the month."

"Well, if she would like the job, here's my contact info." Audrey wrote her name and phone number across the bottom of the penciled sketch and offered it to Janet. "It's only fifteen—maybe twenty—boxes at most. I don't think it would take her much more than a day or so to go through them all. And, as I said, I'll pay well."

"When were you thinking?" Janet asked.

Audrey's shoulders hiked upward. "Sometime this coming week? Monday would be great."

"I'll talk to Tiffany about it at dinner tonight."

"Thank you." Audrey slid her pencil into her handbag and stood. "Though, if she agrees to help, I'll be forced to come up with another reason to treat myself to a piece of your chocolate cream pie on occasion."

Janet rose as well, her gaze lifting from the drawing to the woman responsible for it. "The way I see it, Audrey, there should be no occasion necessary when it comes to pie. Or cookies. Or cake. Or brownies. Or really any baked item, for that matter."

"Then I'll come just because."

Janet tucked the napkin into her pocket and smiled. "Sounds like the perfect reason to me."

**While you are waiting for the next fascinating story
in the Whistle Stop Café Mysteries, check out
some other Guideposts mystery series!**

SAVANNAH SECRETS

Welcome to Savannah, Georgia, a picture-perfect Southern city known for its manicured parks, moss-covered oaks, and antebellum architecture. Walk down one of the cobblestone streets, and you'll come upon Magnolia Investigations. It is here where two friends have joined forces to unravel some of Savannah's deepest secrets. Tag along as clues are exposed, red herrings discarded, and thrilling surprises revealed. Find inspiration in the special bond between Meredith Bellefontaine and Julia Foley. Cheer the friends on as they listen to their hearts and rely on their faith to solve each new case that comes their way.

The Hidden Gate
A Fallen Petal
Double Trouble
Whispering Bells
Where Time Stood Still
The Weight of Years
Willful Transgressions

Season's Meetings
Southern Fried Secrets
The Greatest of These
Patterns of Deception
The Waving Girl
Beneath a Dragon Moon
Garden Variety Crimes
Meant for Good
A Bone to Pick
Honeybees & Legacies
True Grits
Sapphire Secret
Jingle Bell Heist
Buried Secrets
A Puzzle of Pearls
Facing the Facts
Resurrecting Trouble
Forever and a Day

MYSTERIES *of* MARTHA'S VINEYARD

Priscilla Latham Grant has inherited a lighthouse! So with not much more than a strong will and a sore heart, the recent widow says goodbye to her lifelong Kansas home and heads to the quaint and historic island of Martha's Vineyard, Massachusetts. There, she comes face-to-face with adventures, which include her trusty canine friend, Jake, three delightful cousins she didn't know she had, and Gerald O'Bannon, a handsome Coast Guard captain—plus head-scratching mysteries that crop up with surprising regularity.

A Light in the Darkness
Like a Fish Out of Water
Adrift
Maiden of the Mist
Making Waves
Don't Rock the Boat
A Port in the Storm
Thicker Than Water
Swept Away
Bridge Over Troubled Waters
Smoke on the Water
Shifting Sands
Shark Bait
Seascape in Shadows

Storm Tide
Water Flows Uphill
Catch of the Day
Beyond the Sea
Wider Than an Ocean
Sheeps Passing in the Night
Sail Away Home
Waves of Doubt
Lifeline
Flotsam & Jetsam
Just Over the Horizon

MIRACLES & MYSTERIES
of MERCY HOSPITAL

Four talented women from very different walks of life witness the miracles happening around them at Mercy Hospital and soon become fast friends. Join Joy Atkins, Evelyn Perry, Anne Mabry, and Shirley Bashore as, together, they solve the puzzling mysteries that arise at this Charleston, South Carolina, historic hospital—rumored to be under the protection of a guardian angel. Come along as our quartet of faithful friends solve mysteries, stumble upon a few of the hospital's hidden and forgotten passageways, and discover historical treasures along the way! This fast-paced series is filled with inspiration, adventure, mystery, delightful humor, and loads of Southern charm!

Where Mercy Begins
Prescription for Mystery
Angels Watching Over Me
A Change of Art
Conscious Decisions
Surrounded by Mercy
Broken Bonds
Mercy's Healing
To Heal a Heart

A Cross to Bear

Merciful Secrecy

Sunken Hopes

Hair Today, Gone Tomorrow

Pain Relief

Redeemed by Mercy

A Genius Solution

A Hard Pill to Swallow

Ill at Ease

'Twas the Clue Before Christmas

A NOTE FROM the EDITORS

We hope you enjoyed another exciting volume in the Whistle Stop Café Mysteries series, published by Guideposts. For over seventy-five years, Guideposts, a nonprofit organization, has been driven by a vision of a world filled with hope. We aspire to be the voice of a trusted friend, a friend who makes you feel more hopeful and connected.

By making a purchase from Guideposts, you join our community in touching millions of lives, inspiring them to believe that all things are possible through faith, hope, and prayer. Your continued support allows us to provide uplifting resources to those in need. Whether through our communities, websites, apps, or publications, we inspire our audiences, bring them together, and comfort, uplift, entertain, and guide them. Visit us at guideposts.org to learn more.

We would love to hear from you. Write us at Guideposts, P.O. Box 5815, Harlan, Iowa 51593 or call us at (800) 932-2145. Did you love *A String of Pearls*? Leave a review for this product on guideposts.org/shop. Your feedback helps others in our community find relevant products.

Find inspiration, find faith, find Guideposts.

Shop our best sellers and favorites at
guideposts.org/shop

Or scan the QR code to go directly to our Shop

Find more inspiring stories in these best-loved Guideposts fiction series!

Mysteries of Lancaster County

Follow the Classen sisters as they unravel clues and uncover hidden secrets in Mysteries of Lancaster County. As you get to know these women and their friends, you'll see how God brings each of them together for a fresh start in life.

Secrets of Wayfarers Inn

Retired schoolteachers find themselves owners of an old warehouse-turned-inn that is filled with hidden passages, buried secrets, and stunning surprises that will set them on a course to puzzling mysteries from the Underground Railroad.

Tearoom Mysteries Series

Mix one stately Victorian home, a charming lakeside town in Maine, and two adventurous cousins with a passion for tea and hospitality. Add a large scoop of intriguing mystery, and sprinkle generously with faith, family, and friends, and you have the recipe for *Tearoom Mysteries*.

Ordinary Women of the Bible

Richly imagined stories—based on facts from the Bible—have all the plot twists and suspense of a great mystery, while bringing you fascinating insights on what it was like to be a woman living in the ancient world.

To learn more about these books, visit Guideposts.org/Shop